AF496571

Jeffrey A. Lee   Drawings by Leslie Coldrick

Around Historic Yorkshire

MIDAS BOOKS

First published 1978 by
Midas Books
12 Dene Way Speldhurst
Tunbridge Wells Kent TN3 ONX

ISBN 0 85936 109 8

Designed and produced by Mechanick Exercises, London

Printed in Great Britain by Tonbridge Printers Limited,
Peach Hall Works Tonbridge Kent

The Shambles, York

CONTENTS AND ILLUSTRATIONS

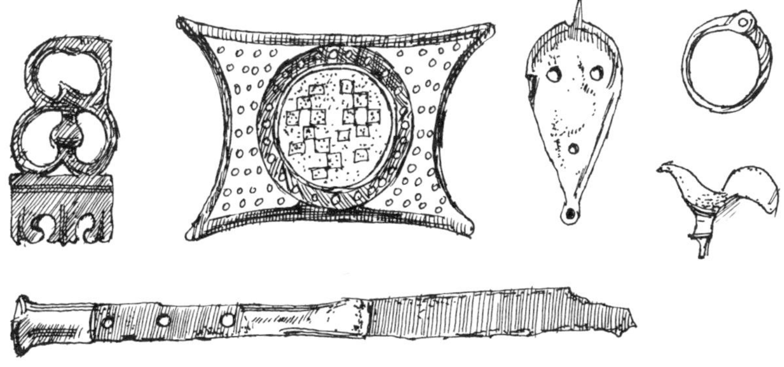

Roman metal objects, found in York

ADWICK-LE-STREET

Visitors from the United States may find the village of Adwick-le-Street near Doncaster of some interest, for it is here that a branch of the Washington family lived. The church opened its doors to the public in 1976 on the two hundredth anniversary of American Independence, and as a tribute to Britain's closest ally in two world wars.

The tomb of James Washington is of particular interest since, on its side, is to be seen the carved family crest involving stars and stripes. It has been claimed that this crest was, indeed, the basis for 'Old Glory', the United States flag.

It is interesting that the man who was appointed Commander in Chief of Continental Forces during the American War of Independence, who received the surrender of Cornwallis in 1781, and who became the first President of the United States in 1789, though he was born in Virginia, should have had his roots and his origins here in the heart of Yorkshire. We might hopefully reflect that the sterling qualities that he showed in his life so conspicuously owed something to his Yorkshire descent.

6

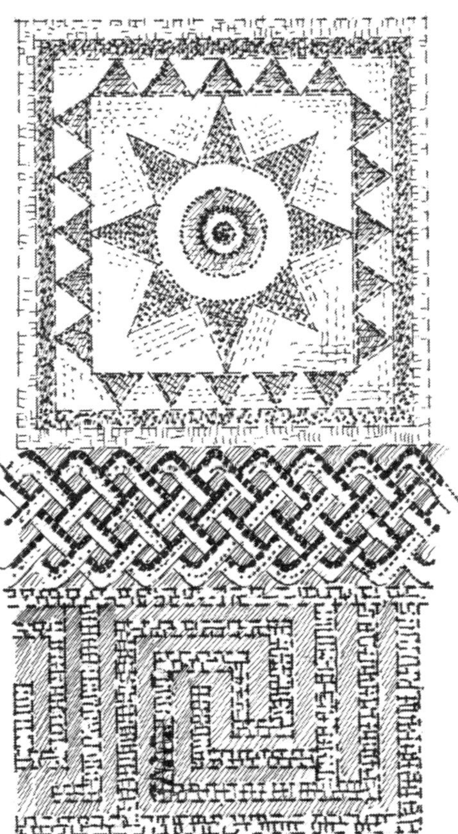

ALDBOROUGH

The village of Aldborough occupies approximately one third of the area once covered by the Roman walled town of Isurium Brigantum. The site of Isurium Brigantum is, however, older than the Roman occupation for, as its name implies, it was originally the capital city of the Brigantes. It is sometimes forgotten that the Romans did not have it all their own way in Britain. Nor were they always the outright victors as the stories of Caradoc and Boudicca make clear. The Brigante Venutius actually defeated a Roman legion under Manlius Valens. Nevertheless, the Romans were extremely methodical and the secret of their success lay in their determination and their unique organizing ability. After the Brigantes had been crushed, the Romans deliberately and wisely, though obviously cruelly, obliterated the Brigante capital and built a Roman town on its site.

Parts of the Roman wall dating from the end of the second century can still be seen on the south western side of the site, where there are also the foundations of two signal towers and a corner tower. In the museum many interesting Brigantian and Roman relics can be seen. The tesselated pavement illustrated is one of five preserved in situ.

ASKRIGG

Askrigg in Wensleydale, home of the famous Wensleydale cheese, goes to some trouble to ensure that the visitor enjoys his stay, for the Askrigg Foundation was set up by a group of local people under the chairmanship of the vicar specifically for that purpose.

One of Askrigg's best recorded villagers was John Harland, born in the village in 1792, the son of a quack doctor who travelled all over Yorkshire. The reason that we know so much about Harland is that, at the age of twenty-one he began a diary that continued almost uninterrupted until 1870, shortly before his death. The impression one gets from reading Harland's diary is that of a man whose human passions frequently clashed with his religious aspirations. He became a convert to Methodism, and in 1811 took his first faltering steps as a preacher. Religious conversion did not quench the fire of physical passion, and, after seducing a young girl named Olivea, he married her on January 8th, 1816. Though they experienced many hardships, the couple were very happy. He records eloquently enough in 1821: "Poverty held us fast in its iron grip. Distress, with his haggard face, seemed to beset me more closely on every side. Clothes were fast wearing out, family increasing, and earnings too scanty to supply present necessities." However, help was at hand. A fellow Methodist, Richard Fawcett, offered Harland work as a warehouseman. Despite this poverty and having reared eight children and lived through the cholera epidemic in Bradford in 1832, Harland managed to survive until he was well on towards eighty.

Nappa Hall

AUSTWICK

Much of the fine scenery in the Dales was sculpted by the ice during the bleak and inhospitable centuries of glaciation some 20,000 years ago, long before man could seek habitation in this terrifying wilderness. During the Ice Age the valleys were filled with solid ice that ground and sculpted such half-egg shaped forms as the drumlins. Evidence of the enormous and relentless force of the ice as it ground its way through the valleys and pushed towards the peaks is demonstrated by the huge blocks of Silurian basement rock that have been carelessly thrust some 400 feet up and, as in the case of Norber Brow, left stranded, as though some terrifying cyclops from the age of giants had picked them up and balanced them like pebbles higher up purely for his own amusement.

Between the intense periods of cold, there were much warmer times, evidence of which have been found in Victoria Cave at Settle: the bones of elephant, of hippopotamus, and of hyena.

Erratic Boulders at Norber Brow

BARDEN TOWER

Barden Tower in Wharfedale, with its tower, its farmhouse, and its chapel, all listed buildings, is of particular historical and architectural interest. Its history has been linked to the lives of two somewhat eccentric aristocratic figures, that of "Shepherd" Lord, Henry Clifford and that of Lady Anne Clifford.

The estate of Barden, so-called from the Anglo-Saxon "Valley of the Wild Bear" was originally granted to Baron Robert de Romille after the Norman conquest, but, until the time of the "Shepherd" Lord, the tower was little more than an exalted hunting lodge.

The "Shepherd" Lord, nicknamed thus because during his childhood at the time of the Wars of the Roses he was hidden among the shepherds of Cumberland, preferred Barden to his castle at Skipton and chose to live there. However, the "Shepherd" was no mean host and was certainly nothing of a recluse. He kept an excellent table by all accounts and entertained on quite a lavish scale. In 1513 the "Shepherd" Lord led a band of his retainers to fight at the Battle of Flodden, which he survived, living until 1523.

Unfortunately, the "Shepherd's" profligate son manifested little interest in Barden Tower and it was not until Lady Anne Clifford took possession, after many legal wrangles, in 1643 that the long overdue repairs and extensions were put in hand. In her old age Lady Anne rejoiced in visiting her numerous properties with full pomp and state, travelling in a horse litter and accompanied by gentlewomen, officials and servants sometimes numbering as many as 300 souls.

BEAMSLEY

One of the most important families in Wharfedale was the Clifford family, very well-known for their acts of benevolence and their sense of personal responsibility for all those in their employ. Most famous of the Cliffords was Lady Anne who fought a vigorous and perhaps somewhat piratical battle with Lady Elizabeth Clifford for the possession of Barden Tower, the home she loved so dearly. Lady Margaret, Anne's mother, built Beamsley Hospital in 1593, as the inscription inside assures us. It was in concentric form with five rooms or "houses radiating from the small central chapel. Residence was restricted to the widows of men who had rendered service at Skipton Castle, the Clifford Family seat. Each widow, living independently in her "house" was nevertheless required to attend services in the chapel, and, on their side, the Family guaranteed the continuance of facilities for regular worship. Lady Anne continued and extended her mother's work by providing six more cottages connected to the main almshouses by an arch. Correspondence referring to residencies in the almshouses can still be seen at Skipton Castle. In 1960 the Charity Commissioners took over the running of the almshouses, and in 1961 improvements were carried out which reduced the number of places from thirteen to eight, though with greatly improved facilities. Though the chapel has been largely refurbished, what is believed to be the original candelabrum remains together with a portrait of Lady Anne.

Beamsley Hospital

BEVERLEY MINSTER

There are three parish churches in Beverley, a town of fewer than 18,000 inhibitants, and two of these churches, St Mary's and Beverley Minster, are extremely fine, bearing testimony to the town's long and distinguished ecclesiastical associations. Before the Reformation, there were two principal powers in Beverley, that of the Archbishop of York, who governed approximately the north end of the borough, and that of the Provost and Canons of Beverley Minster, who ruled the south end. This may, indeed, account for the fact that there are two markets in the town to this day.

However, during the reign of Henry VIII both powers were drastically reduced, leaving Beverley in a state of decline. The men of Beverley were among the first to protest against Henry's oppressive measures. Indeed, one of the martyrs of his reign, Bishop John Fisher of Rochester, had been a pupil at Beverley Grammar School. Another local man, one Robert Aske of Aughton, called upon the citizens of Beverley to protest against the forcible closing of the smaller monasteries. "The Pilgrimage of Grace", as it was called, was strongly supported by the men of Humberside. The movement was so powerful that it extracted promises of redress from the King, but, as soon as the rebels had been disbanded, Henry went back on his promises and hanged the leaders, including Aske, from gibbets as a warning to others.

Elizabeth I went some way to make amends, for in 1573 she granted the town its charter, expressing the pious hope that it be allowed to remain "a town of peace and quiet". She might have added of graciousness and much beauty.

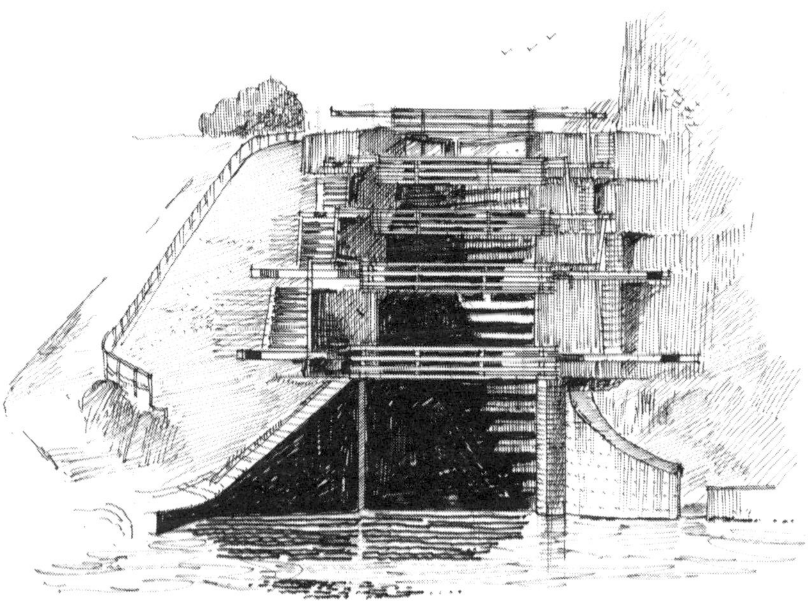

BINGLEY

The Five Rise Locks situated half way between Micklethwaite Bridge and Three Rise Locks were considered by many in the eighteenth century to be one of the world's leading engineering feats, and are still well worth viewing with admiration for the intrepid builders of the Liverpool-Leeds Canal. The Canal itself was begun by the engineer John Longbotham and the stretch between Bingley and Skipton was opened on April 7th, 1773. It was not until 1816, however, that the whole one hundred and twenty seven miles of canal was completed with ninety-one locks and three hundred bridges at what would be considered today the extremely modest price of £1,200,000. Now only leisure cruisers and the odd coal barge make their 4 m.p.h way along it whereas in its heyday it conveyed two million tons of freight annually.

There is a difference of sixty feet between the upper and lower pools of Five Rise Locks. Each lock is twelve feet deep and is capable of passing boats of sixty feet long and fourteen feet wide.

The town of Bingley, astride the River Aire and the Canal, owes its earlier prosperity to textiles. It contains some interesting sixteenth and seventeenth century buildings, while, at the corner of Millgate stands the much older 'White Horse Inn'. Millgate leads to Ireland Bridge, beside which stands the old corn mill, now used as a forge.

BIRSTALL

Birstall played an important part in the history of Methodism in Yorkshire, for it was here in 1741 that John Nelson, a stonemason, established the first society. By 1743 no fewer than twenty-three meeting houses had been established. However, Wesley and his followers were not always welcome. Though many of the clergy, particularly the incumbent of Huddersfield, were encouraging, others tended to see Methodists as rivals. In spite of persecution, Methodism flourished in Yorkshire until by 1770 it was possibly the most Methodist county in England.

Birstall can also claim with some pride to be the birthplace of one of the most original and fearless thinkers of the eighteenth century, Joseph Priestley. He was born into the family of a Calvinist weaver, and while serving as minister at Mill Hill Chapel in Leeds he evinced an interest in the brewery next door, though he gained less satisfaction from the beer than from the process of fermentation that preceeded it. One chemical interest led to another, until Priestley made his great discovery — oxygen.

Priestley was very much aware of the conflict between science and religion, and in 1774 he wrote "Letters to a Philosophical Unbeliever" to demolish the fallacy that science and religion are incompatible. He was also sympathetic to the political motives behind the French Revolution, and it was during a meeting to celebrate the Fall of the Bastille, that his house was set on fire by a mob and destroyed. Priestley became disenchanted with his own country and emigrated to the United States where he lived until his death in 1804, although he remained a British citizen until the end.

14

BOLTON ABBEY

The West Door, which admits into the nave of Bolton Abbey, exhibits
work that is typical of the Early English Period, the design regular,
comparatively free from ornamentation, and without variation. But, of
course, like most Medieval buildings, Bolton presents one with an amalgam
of styles from Norman to Perpendicular.

The Augustinians came to the site in 1154 from Embsay, where their
community had been established by William Mechin and his wife Cecilia de
Rumilly in 1120. They dedicated the Abbey to the Blessed Virgin and to
Saint Cuthbert.

Yorkshire frequently found itself in the Scottish invaders who bore
down from the North with fire and flailing sword against all who stood in
their way. In 1320 Bolton Abbey was attacked and was so badly damaged
that the canons had to be temporarily dispersed to other houses so that
repairs could be carried out.

At the time of the surrender of the house to King Henry VIII in 1540
there were fourteen canons and the Prior.

BOROUGHBRIDGE

At Boroughbridge, a town well-known for its sheep auctions, are to be seen three mysterious reminders of man's distant and veiled past, "The Devil's Arrows", as they are called. Legend has it that in one of his rages Satan let fly with a barrage of arrows, probably intending to wreak havoc upon the people of York or Ripon and that by the intervention of the angels he missed his target.

It is believed that originally there were five of these monoliths standing almost in a straight line, separated from one another by approximately one hundred yards, the tallest being perhaps thirty feet high. Each of the stones is grooved and scarred from the top down with strange and obscure markings as though the Devil had whittled them with a giant blade before hurling them down. These "Devil's Arrows" of millstone grit probably date from 2000 to 1,500 B.C., but nobody can now be certain of their date or purpose. Were they hauled some ten miles and erected by a race of super mathematicians, or are they phallic symbols associated with a remote fertility religion? Perhaps we shall never know for sure. One thing, however seems certain: the stones standing erect and potent with a mysterious power near Boroughbridge do mark a site that was regarded by Bronze Age man as sacred.

The Devil's Arrows

BOWES

According to local belief the village of Bowes made an unintentional and perhaps not entirely welcome contribution to literature for it was after a visit to the village that Charles Dickens wrote "Nicholas Nickleby" which included the infamous school of Dotheboys Hall and its scoundrelly headmaster Squeers. There was indeed a school known as Shaw's Academy in the village run by a certain William Shaw, whose grave is in the churchyard. Local opinion has it that Shaw gave Dickens a somewhat abrupt and discourteous reception when the great novelist asked to look over the school, with the result that Dickens converted Shaw into the disagreeable Squeers. Whether Shaw's Academy was as dubious a place of education as Dickens makes it in "Nicholas Nickleby" is difficult to assess. The church register confirms that there were a number of deaths among pupils during Dickens's time, and, in the churchyard, not far from Shaw's grave there is another grave that is reputed to be that of the boy whom Dickens took as his model for Smike!

If Shaw was maligned it is a pity, though the achievement of "Nicholas Nickleby" pleads eloquently for Dickens' forgiveness.

Dotheboys Hall

BRADFORD 1

Like that of many towns and cities of the North Bradford's rise to
eminence began somewhat late. It appears in the Domesday Book only as a
waste worth nothing, probably because of the effect of William the
Conqueror's destructive interdict. By the time of the Civil War, however,
the textile trade was flourishing. The citizens of Bradford favoured the
Parliamentary cause and, because of this, the City was besieged in 1642
and in 1643, when it was taken by the Royalist forces. The citizens
ingeniously protected their parish church, now Bradford Cathedral, from
the depredations of the enemy cannon by hanging woolsacks about it.

After the fall of the city, the Earl of Newcastle set up his headquarters
in the Bolling Hall. There is a legend which says that, as the Royalist
commander contemplated putting certain of the citizens to the sword, he
was visited by a ghost which managed to prevail upon his conscience.

Though the citizens were saved, Bradford continued to suffer: Civil War
and Plague drastically reduced its prosperity, and it did not begin to
recover until the late eighteenth century with the rise of the Industrial
Revolution.

The Bolling Hall

BRADFORD 2

Fittingly enough Bradford has recorded the history of its own textile industry by establishing the Bradford Industrial Museum in a building that was actually in use as a spinning mill until 1970. The collection gives a composite picture of the development of textiles from the earliest times to the present day and includes a large variety of textile machinery. However, there are also many other interesting exhibits including a fine transport section with early bicycles and carriages, not forgetting, of course, examples of the exclusively Bradford product, the Jowett motorcar.

Ben and Willie Jowett shared a devotion to quality in their cars so that their production remained at no more than twenty-five vehicles per week until 1935, each car being the result of individual craftsmanship. The Long Saloon, their first family car, appeared in 1928. It was capable of 47 m.p.g. and was particularly good at hill climbing, frequently leaving behind much more prestigious models. After the Second World War, Jowetts produced a series of excellent cars, including the famous Jowett Javelin, a 13 horse power car capable of 80 m.p.h. This was followed by the Jowett Jupiter which won the Monte Carlo Rally in the 1½ litre class.

Unfortunately, though Jowetts were excellent cars, the company could not withstand the pressures of a highly competitive world, and, in 1954, it was taken over by International Harvesters. In big business, alas, the best do not always survive!

BRADFORD 3

We read a great deal about the callousness and lack of concern for the welfare of workpeople among the industrial entrepreneurs during the last century but there were some men of conscience among them who cared about the welfare of those upon whose labours they depended for their wealth. Eminent among them was Sir Titus Salt who built a "model" village to accommodate eight hundred and fifty of the families in his employ. Sir Titus's intention was to centre a whole ideal community round his alpaca wool mill, which he opened in 1953.

The dining-room of his village provided cheap meals with meat dishes for as little as 2d, while the Congregational church, to which he gave his allegiance, provided for the people's spiritual needs. Sir Titus, however, was also interested in developing the cultural interests of his employees and a social centre and library were set up to this end.

Disapproving of the evils of drink, he refused to allow a public house to be erected in Saltaire, and he set a disagreeably arduous example to his workpeople by always arriving at the mill long before anybody else.

As Mayor of Bradford, during a period of severe unemployment at the time of the cholera epidemic, he opened soup kitchens and took on a hundred men though he had no need of their services.

The houses of Saltaire, built in stone in the Italian style are undoubtedly a monument to a man who cared about people in an age when it was often easier not to bother.

BRADFORD 4

Standing severe and uncompromising in the bad taste of its Italianate
Gothic pride, Bradford's Wool Exchange, built in 1868, at the height of
the city's prosperity, is a solid monument to the wealth and confidence of
the Victoian Age. Indeed, Bradford's influence among towns was minimal
until the introduction of the Spinning Jenny in 1790. From that day
Bradford's wealth increased phenomenally. In 1820 there were twenty
woollen mills within the city, but by 1873 this number had increased to
200. During this period the population rose from 13,000 to 183,000. The
first railway linking Bradford to Leeds was built in 1847.

Though Bradford owes most of its prosperity to wool, we must not
forget the names of its distinguished citizens who have contributed so
notably to the arts, among them the composer Delius, Sir John
Rothenstein, the art critic, David Hockney, the painter, and that most
specific and unpretentious of Yorkshire writers J. B. Priestley.

BRIDLINGTON

In the Domesday Book Bridlington appears as Bretlington though certain other documents and charters dating from the twelfth century refer to it as Berlington. No one is certain of the origin of the name, though it probably stems from an early settler named Bretel or Bertell.

Bridlington gained some prominence during the reign of Henry I with the foundation of an Augustinian house by Walter de Gant. The monastery was, however, dissolved and largely destroyed in 1537. Bridlington began to develop as a market town about one and a half miles from the sea, governed by the Lords Feoffees until 1863. At about that time the centre of interest shifted towards the sea and, with the building of Royal Prince's Parade in 1867 at a cost of £20,000 Bridlington was established as a seaside resort. To gain some understanding of this enterprise we have to realise not only that the pound was worth considerably more in 1867 than it is today but also that in 1867 the population of Bridlington was a mere 6,000. In fact Bridlington has spent more than any other resort of comparable size on the construction and maintenance of its sea-defences. Between 1879 and 1880 the Alexandra Sea Wall was constructed, while between 1887 and 1888 considerable sums were spent on Beaconsfield Sea Wall.

Today Bridlington has much to offer the holidaymaker as one of Yorkshire's most attractive seaside holiday centres.

BRIDLINGTON 2

Large enterprises are often said to have small beginnings, and there is evidence for this in Applegarth Lane, Bridlington where a church twelve feet square, with a single low door, one window, and a pantiled roof modestly stands. Every September a little group of local Baptists meet here for a commemoration service to mark the anniversary of the building of this tiny church in 1698.

The Baptist church in Yorkshire had an almost biblical genesis. A certain Scottish farmer had become a convicted Baptist while visiting London. On his journey home, however, his ship was assailed by a fearful storm and he was forced ashore in Bridlington Bay. The farmer immediately interpreted this as a vocational sign and thus was born the Baptist Church in Bridlington.

Though there were originally only twenty one members of this Baptist community, within a century and a quarter, the Baptist faith had spread widely over the East and North Ridings.

In the church one can still see the original minute book with its first minute dated 16th September, 1698. In the minute the first members, all of them named, dedicate themselves to the service of Christ in the Baptist Faith. At the top of the list is the name of the first pastor, Robert Purdom. Purdom served as Pastor for ten years and, when he died in 1708, his body was buried beside the church. To this day one can still see his named carved into the crumbling stone on the wall.

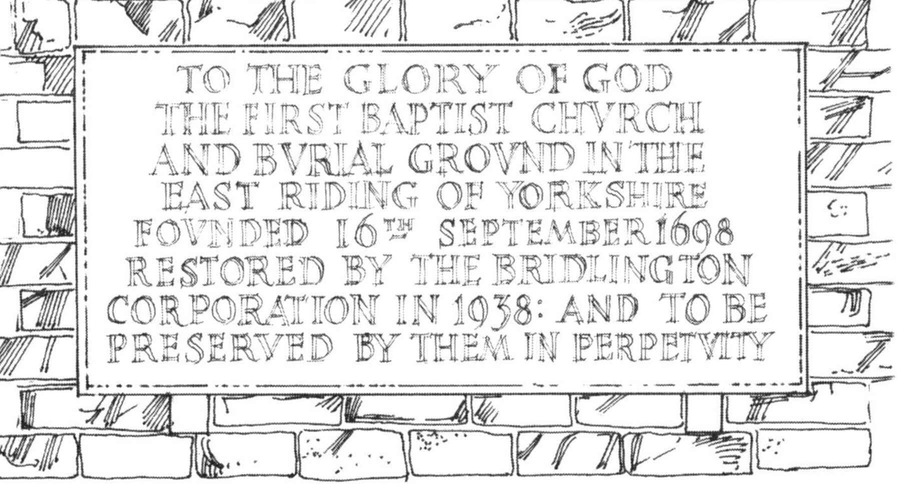

BRIGHOUSE

Brighouse was quite a modest village until 1759 when the Calder and Hebble navigation was opened. Even in 1859 it was described on a tablet locally as 'a hamlet', though, by that time such a description must have been somewhat over-modest. The town was appointed a borough in 1893. In the nineteenth century, at least until 1851, it had quite an impressive jail and the last man to be imprisoned in it must have been something of a wag as is revealed by the contrast between his name, Peter Ratcliffe, and his alias, Peter Fox. It was the stones of the demolished jail that were used to build the "bellissima" or Victoria Tower, which gives an excellent view over the Calder and the Lower Shibden Valleys.

The mention of outlaws reminds us that in 1936 a bridegroom arrived at St Martin's, the parish church, only to find a posse of law enforcement officers waiting to arrest him, scarcely a happy deliverance except from the least felicitous of marriage prospects! Robin Hood is, of course, well-known in these parts. His sister is reputed to have been the Abbess of Kirklees Priory and it is there, not far away, that the ubiquitous outlaw is said to have been laid to rest, but we must not leave Brighouse before reminding ourselves that this is the country of brass bands, not the least of which is the Brighouse and Rastrick Band with its excellent reputation among brass band lovers.

Brighouse Gallery

BRIMHAM ROCKS

An important centre of interest to the tourist, attracting no fewer than 60,000 visitors a year and owned now by the National Trust, is the strange collection of grotesquely configurated rocks known as Brimham Rocks. Nobody knows for sure how these rocks became so fantastically sculpted. Wind erosion is no doubt partly to blame though the names of one or two of the poised or logan-stones, "The Wigg Stones" and "Jenny Twigg" suggested an interesting association. Can "Wig" be derived from "Wicca", meaning "Wiseman"? For that matter, where does the name "Brimham" come from? It has been suggested that the name is really either the Old English "beam" or "tree", or that it is "byrne" meaning "brown". Does it, perhaps, echo an ancient historical association with the tree Yggdrasill of Scandinavian mythology? Yggdrasill is "The World Tree". This wonderful creative tree, mother of all living things, spreads through the length and breath of the universe. Its roots go right down into the heart of the earth. Its branches stretch to the very limits of the sky. In the shadow of its leaves all animals and birds are nourished, and, though they feed constantly, the Tree is never exhausted because it is eternally regenerated by the Well of Urn, the Fountain of Eternal Youth.

CASTLE HOWARD

Fifteen miles north-east of York near the village of Conysthorpe in the
Howardian Hills stands one of the finest of England's great houses built in
the eighteenth century by the architect and dramatist Sir John Vanburgh,
who lived between 1664 and 1726. Vanburgh, a man of handsome
appearance, jovial, and of considerable popularity was of Flemish descent.
His father, a merchant of Ghent had fled to England after persecution at
the hands of the Duke of Alva. Vanburgh himself was a prisoner in the
Bastille in 1691 suspected of spying. In England he was much honoured.
George I knighted him, and from 1704 until his death he served as
Clarenceaux king-of-arms.

Among the other buildings designed by this brilliant architect are
Blenheim Palace, Dalkeith Palace, and The Haymarket, his own theatre.

Castle Howard, built in the Baroque style which Vanburgh and his
contemporary Nicholas Hawksmoor made famous, is of heroic proportions
and seems to demand as its inhabitants a race of Olympians. It rests
superbly in extensive landscaped grounds.

CAWTHORNE

Cawthorne, a few miles to the west of Barnsley, is considered to be one of South Yorkshire's most attractive villages. It contains a number of interesting and historic buildings, including the Parish Room and the Red House. Near the gate of the nineteenth-century church, into which have been built a number of Saxon stones, stand the remains of a Saxon cross.

Near the village in a seventy-acre park is the mansion known as Cannon Hall, once the home of the Spencer Stanhope family. Cannon Hall was built in the seventeenth century but was largely remodelled at about 1765 by the well-known architect Carr of York. Inside the mansion is housed an art gallery and the regimental museum of the Thirteenth and Eighteenth Hussars. Among the exhibits is a diorama of the famous Charge of the Light Brigade, that heroic but costly blunder of the Crimean War in which the Thirteenth Hussars plunged towards the Russian batteries with such enormous losses. Out of the six hundred men who, because of a misunderstood order, charged against an overwhelming and heavily armed enemy force, only two hundred survived. Not for the first or the last time had the British soldier's courage shown itself to be superior to the crass stupidity of higher command.

Cannon Hall

CHAPEL-LE-DALE

Chapel-le-Dale in its U-shaped valley below Ingleborough and Simon Fell reminds those with an interest in local history of the navvies or "navigators", that hardy and independent race of men who drove the Settle-Carlisle Railway up across Ribblehead between 1869 and 1876. A particularly difficult part of the line was on Blea Moor where a tunnel was constructed in the most treacherous conditions. These men and their women lived tough, hard-drinking lives in shanty towns with outlandish names like Jericho, Sebastopol, Inkerman, Belgravia, Salt Lake City and Batty Green, reminiscent of the Wild West. Their off duty interests, apart from strenuous drinking bouts, included dog racing, cock-fighting and bare fisted fighting. It was not unheard of for a navvy to sell his wife, as Henchard did in "The Mayor of Casterbridge", for the sake of a gallon of beer. Six thousand navvies were employed to drive the railway up across the fells and, of these, as many as two hundred died of accidents, fever and the terrible outbreaks of smallpox. The church of St Leonards actually had to enlarge its graveyard to accommodate one hundred bodies from the shanty towns. In its dark interior there is a marble plaque erected at the expense of the Midland Railway Company to the memory of those men, women, and children who sacrificed their lives to the greedy iron god of the rail.

CLAPHAM

Clapham is one of the most popular tourist centres in the Dales and evidence for this is provided by the Manor House which is now used as the National Park Information Centre. The Manor House was restored in 1890 but it was originally completed in 1701. Inside is a very fine eighteenth century fireplace with a span of eleven feet; a great comfort before the days of central heating!

The history of Clapham has been largely dominated by the fortunes of the Farrer family for it was Oliver Farrer who bought the shooting rights and created an estate stretching to the head of Ribblesdale. Everyone who has read Jane Austen's "Mansfield Park" knows of the nineteenth century's passion for "improvements", and Clapham was not to escape, for the Farrers redesigned the whole of the north end of the village and dammed Clapham Beck to create a lake that covered eight acres and held forty-eight and a half million gallons of water.

Ingleborough Caves, just north of the village, were opened by the Farrers as an attraction in the 1830s. Here begins a vast system of caverns which links with Gaping Gill, and includes the largest underground cavity in Britain. There is some difference of opinion as to who first descended Gaping Gill, one of the principal pot-holes in the country. The modern tourist is lowered in the comparative comfort and safety of a bosun's chair in approximately ninety seconds!

CONISBROUGH CASTLE

The most interesting feature of Conisbrough Castle, four miles south west of Doncaster, is its massive and unique cylindrical keep which stands ninety-five feet high and is supported by six splendid buttresses. The person responsible for this monumental departure from the usual Norman rectangular keep was Hamelin Plantagenet, half brother of Henry II. The keep is entered by the first floor, and there is a ladder leading down into a vaulted storeroom below, which also contains the castle's well. On the second floor is the hall, and, above this, on the third floor is the lord's bedchamber, and, set into one of the buttresses, the Castle Chapel.

From the watchturret above, the Castle enjoys extensive views over the surrounding countryside.

Because most of the Castle had been neglected and allowed to fall into a state of severe dilapidation, it attracted little attention from either side during the Civil War. It is for this reason that the keep stands so well preserved to this day. Looking at it one can understand immediately why Sir Walter Scott chose it as the setting for "Ivanhoe".

The Keep

COXWOLD

Coxwold has been justly described as one of the most gracious towns in Yorkshire. Above its wide street, edged with lawns stands the beautiful perpendicular church of St. Michael's with its fine octagonal tower.

Nearby is "Shandy Hall", an old gabled brick house which served as the home of the curate, the novelist Laurence Sterne from 1760 until his death in 1768.

Sterne was a strange and eccentric character somewhat in advance of his time. He enjoyed a large circle of boisterous and rowdy friends with whom he frequently went shooting and whom he entertained dextrously on his fiddle, all this apparently reconciled with his priestly vocation.

He published "Tristram Shandy" in London in 1760, a work which achieved an instant success because of its indelicacy, though it must have puzzled his contemporaries with its surrealistic association of images and the thinness of its plot.

"Sentimental Journey", published in the year of his death, a work much easier to follow, also achieved a considerable success.

Much of Sterne's time, after the publication of "Tristram Shandy" was spent, either living it up in London or abroad in search of better health. He died practically penniless in his lodgings in Old Bond Street.

Shandy Hall

DENT

This very beautiful village with cobbled streets in the heart of Dentdale is famous above all things for its knitting. The women of Dentdale, however, were no ordinary knitters; Robert Southey paid them a considerable tribute when he referred to them in his novel "The Doctor" as "terrible". They were terrible in the very best sense meaning that they were without compare. In older times the local wool had been spun into very coarse threads which produced a material known as bump, but, in about 1840 when William and Mary Howitt took up residence in the valley, the domestic knitting industry entered a period of unprecedented vigour. Adam Sedgwick, Dent's most famous son, commemorated by the granite slab in the main street, describes how, during the winters' evenings whole families, mothers, children, aunts, grandmothers, etc. congregated for a knitting season round the peat hearth, like so many wizened witches, swaying rhythmically and making a fine din that was compounded of knitting sticks, "wires" and chatter. The knitters of Dent had devised their own quite distinctive methods, involving the use of a dagger like tool or knitting-stick, and curved needles known as "wires" or"pricks". While knitting, both hands were used at once in what has been described as a tossing motion. When a young man became engaged to a young girl of the village it was the custom for him to present her with a specially fashioned knitting stick. These knitting sticks are now treasured relics and museum pieces.

Adam Sedgwick's Stone

DEWSBURY

In a deep hollow that was once a glacial lake lies the town of Dewsbury. Its history goes back at least as far as the Romans, for in no fewer than three places on higher ground hoards of Roman coins have been discovered: at Thornhill, at Dewsbury Moor and in Crow Nest Park. Dewsbury began to thrive, however, after the departure of the Romans. In the ninth century the town possessed a magnificent eighteen foot cross, carved elaborately and having the figures of Christ and the apostles at its base. This cross, described by Henry VIII's antiquarian Leland and dubbed "The Pauline Cross", has now unfortunately disappeared and only a few fragments remain, though a reconstruction of it exists in Tolson Museum in Huddersfield.

Dewsbury Market, open on Tuesdays and Saturdays, was first established as early as 1318.

Dewsbury has what some people might regard as the dubious honour of being the home of "Shoddy", though "shoddy", the art of recycling textile material invented by Benjamin Law in 1813, is by no means to be despised. The "shoddy" trade was greatly boosted after the Crimean War (1853-1856) with the return of soldiers' uniforms. Fibres are most carefully sorted and graded, and "shoddy" materials, when mixed with newer fibres are actually said to spin better.

DONCASTER

Little now remains to supply evidence of Doncaster's importance in the life of Roman Britain or of the part it played in the wars between the rival York and Lancaster factions. There is, however, a symbol of Doncaster's immense civic pride preserved and cherished in its distinctive Georgian Mansion House.

The Mansion House, one of only three civic mansions remaining in the country, was built in 1740 according to a design by Thomas Paine. The striking features of this powerful and forthright statement in painted stone are its paired Corinthian columns and its central Venetian window with flanking pedimented lights.

An attic, quite in keeping with the original design, was added by William Lindley of York in 1801. On the skyline is a sculptured lion from Doncaster's armorial bearings.

Visitors in search of Doncaster's Georgian past are advised to go and look at South Parade where they will see a number of other splendid listed Georgian buildings. They might also care to look at the Market Place, at French Gate, and at St George's Gate.

Doncaster's importance to the punter and to those who love horse-racing is indicated by its racecourse on the east side of the town. The eighteenth century grandstand is of particular interest.

DRIFFIELD

Driffield's development has been determined by its position and role as the centre of the largely agricultural Wolds area. Its main industries have been those allied to agriculture: the milling of corn, the malting of barley, the brewing of beer, and the manufacture and repair of agricultural implements. Within a radius of six miles of the town there are still the remains of four windmills, the best preserved being at Hutton Cranswick. However, with the tendency towards centralization during the last century, Driffield expanded as a centre for grain milling, with the production of larger steam-driven mills that were more powerful than either wind or water-mills, the first of these being Albion Mill, built in 1846 during the same year as the railway was opened to Driffield. During this time, the town also contained a number of excellent breweries, all of which have now unfortunately vanished because of competition with the bigger city breweries and their vastly inferior product. As the breweries declined, however, maltings such as Skerne Road Malting were built, or converted from other purposes, so that barley could be malted locally before being sent to the breweries. Skerne Road Maltings, perhaps some-what fittingly, presents its better face to the railway which was its closest friend and helpmeet. Its long brick wall is divided by pilasters into thirteen bays, and on each of three floors of each bay is a small opening. At the centre of the Maltings is a rather splendid sack-hoist. Sad to report, the Maltings ceased to function as a maltings in 1962, since when it has served as a store for grain.

Skerne Road Maltings

DRYSTONE WALL

Drystone walling is one of the features of rural Yorkshire, particularly in the area covered by the Yorkshire Dales, where walls feature prominently in the landscape and tell their tales of history to the discriminating eye. Some of the earliest sections of wall go back as far as Romano-British times. Walling was used extensively by the monks of Rievaulx, Jervaulx and Bolton Abbey in medieval times, and one can find many sections of wall that were originally built to enclose centuries-old common fields.

When the greed for land was rampant during the eighteenth and nineteenth centuries and the acts of enclosure permitted landlords to enclose vast areas of land supposedly in the interests of agricultural efficiency, much drystone walling ensued, many of the walls running straight as a die in defiance both of contour and human feelings. The very people who laboured to complete the walls were in many cases those that they pauperized and dispossessed.

Drystone walls still play an important part in providing shelter and enclosures for stock on hillsides, though drystone walling, an expensive and highly skilled craft has like many other country crafts fallen into neglect.

EARBY

"We're bound to slavery for four pence a day." Such were the words of an old Yorkshire leadminer. His life was desperately hard and there were few pleasures. He was of interest to no man in his day except as a drudge. How surprised he would be were he to come back for an afternoon and visit the oldest building in Earby, the Old Grammer School, now devoted entirely to recording the life and work of the old lead miners. The Earby Mine Research Group is bent upon restoring as many of the old mine-workings as may be rendered safe and sturdy. Together with the Cross Hills Naturalist Society it has, for example, restored the smelt chimney on Malham Moor with the judicious use of a fair quantity of cement. Most interesting of all, however, are the exhibits in the Museum, many small items depicting the life of the average miner: clay pipes from Wensleydale and Arkengarthdale, candles used long ago in the workings, and, perhaps, above all miners' boots, strangely twisted and bent, reminding one of the boots in Van Gogh's well-known painting. Also, are to be seen the tools of the trade: picks, shovels, an air fan that worked by hand, axes and clevis hooks. Everything that is human is of interest, even the poor miner who slaved under the earth for his humble four pence a day.

The Old Grammar School

FILEY

The small resort of Filey is a mixture of the old and new. Largely unspoilt by over-exploitation, it still retains much of the charm of an old fishing town: the colourful fishing-vessels lined up on the beach; the fishermen at work on their nets; six miles of glorious sandy beach. It was here that Charlotte Bronte enjoyed a number of holidays.

Among the achievements of Filey is the record of its splendid lifeboat service. There was an official lifeboat service in the town as early as 1823. The old lifeboat was replaced in 1852 by a newer, more up-to-date lifeboat: thirty feet long, with a ten foot beam, and six pairs of oars; but with little hope of being righted after a capsize. At this time the first lifeboat house was erected. There are records on view in the present life-boat house dating back to April 172th, 1854 when the lifeboat put to sea as the sloop "Comet" of Whitby foundered. Despite its limitations the lifeboatmen managed to save four lives.

A series of lifeboats has been used since that date, not the least of which was the "Hollon the Third", launched on April 3rd, 1907. This boat served for thirty years, was launched one hundred and ten times, and rescued one hundred and twenty-one people.

In 1966 the inshore lifeboat service was introduced, and, within seven years, no fewer than forty-five people had been saved from drowning. This historic work of mercy is often taken for granted but it is no less heroic for all that.

Inshore Lifeboat

FLAMBOROUGH LIGHTHOUSE

Those who approach Flamborough Head by way of the massive Iron Age earthwork known as Danes' Dyke must have a good head for heights.

Before one reaches the present lighthouse one passes an octagonal, dressed-chalk tower, patched with red bricks. This is all that remains of the former lighthouse, built at about 1673 by Sir John Clayton, a local entrepreneur who recouped his financial outlay by collecting dues from ships passing the headland. How he achieved this remarkable feat is not recorded, though it must have been an uncertain and possibly hazardous undertaking at the best.

The inadequacy of Sir John's light led to an unfortunate number of shipwrecks, and, in 1806, a public-spirited Custom and Excise man named Benjamin Milne urged that a new lighthouse be built. The man chosen as both architect and builder was a certain John Matson who had lived a life of great hardship as a pressed man in the Navy and as a soldier in the Indian Army. Matson built the lighthouse, which rises to 85 feet, without scaffolding, in the amazingly short time of five months.

The lighthouse stands 214 feet above the sea level and its light can be seen at a distance of 21 miles. During misty or foggy weather two blasts are sounded on the foghorn every one and a half minutes.

FOUNTAINS ABBEY

In 1132 thirteen Cistercian monks who had become dissatisfied with what they considered to be the slackness of their order in York decided to move to a new site near Ripon and found what was to become the wealthiest of the Cistercian houses in England. The wealth of the Abbey was built upon wool, and its interests soon spread far and wide in the County.

In the thirteenth century the abbots spent a great deal of time disputing with rival foundations such as those of Bolton and Salley over their rightful boundaries, and there was much erecting of limestone walls in areas such as Malham Moor. Many of the drystone walls still seen today have stood more or less in their present form for centuries, though it is to be regretted that the true craft of drystone walling is now almost dead.

Fountains Abbey, situated in a beautiful green valley three miles east of Ripon, is a truly impressive ruin, basically of transitional Norman work as the fine West doorway attests. Other features worthy of note are the vaulting of the cellarium and the magnificent cloister arches. The tower, built by the Abbots Huby and Darnlon in the fifteenth century is a well-preserved example of the perpendicular style.

When one visits the Abbey one must not forget to look at Fountains Hall, the fine Jacobean house, excellently furnished, that stands at the entrance to the Abbey.

GIGGLESWICK

Looking across Settle from Castleberg towards Giggleswick, one of the first things of interest that one notices is the dome of the public school, copper-covered but now, of course, oxidized to an attractive turquoise green. The dome was constructed as a memorial of the 1897 jubilee at the behest and expense of Walter Morrison of Malham Tarn one of whose principal enthusiasms was the archaeology of Palestine. The architect, Thomas G. Jackson, took up the challenge with delight for it is not every day that an architect has the privilege of constructing a dome. Though purists objected, for this is their principal role, Jackson felt that his blending of the dome with the Gothic character of the School was not unfelicitous.
and in 1552 Edward VI granted a royal charter by which it became a free grammar school with an endowment of land in the East Riding.

The Dales village of Giggleswick, within easy reach of fell and crag, probably originally Gikel-wick, a Saxon settlement, contains many attractive buildings, and is a delightful place to visit.

GLAISDALE

On the bridge at Glaisdale are carved the initials of Thomas Ferres who is reputed to have had it built in the year 1621. Known variously as "Lover's Bridge" and "Beggar's Bridge", Glaisdale Bridge has an interesting story. As a young impecunious tramp Ferres is said to have had an assignation on the opposite bank of the river with a girl with whom he was passionately in love. Unfortunately, on the night of the proposed tryst Ferres was prevented from meeting his paramour since the river was in full flood. Some reports suggest that Ferres gave up only after the most strenuous efforts and after almost drowning in the river. At any rate he took an oath there and then that, when he should become rich, he would build a bridge across the Esk so that future lovers could avoid similar frustration of the course of true love. Ferres kept his pledge, for years after this event he became wealthy and was made Mayor of Hull. Nobody claims to know how many times he subsequently crossed "Lover's Bridge" himself, or indeed what happened to the lady who had inspired his passion.

The Bridge

GRANTLEY HALL

Another example of a great enterprise which had a small beginning is
Grantley Hall situated about five miles to the west of Ripon. The mansion
built in the later half of the eighteenth century in the Adam style
dominates and tends to overshadow completely the much more modest
house built by Thomas Norton in the last decade of the seventeenth
century. Norton, a member of a once rich and influential family that had
been ruined because of its participation in the Rising of the North of
1569, built the original Grantley Hall when the fortunes of his family were
at their lowest ebb. In the next generation but one, however, the family
fortunes began to revive when Thomas's grandson, Fletcher Norton, an
aggressive and forthright Yorkshireman of the traditional type, became an
M.P. and later the Speaker of the House of Commons. A large bell on top
of the coach house erected to summon the estate workers has the date
1777 which gives a possible clue to the date of the extension of the
mansion. Grantley Hall stands in the midst a most beautiful thirty-acre
estate and is now used as a college. One curious feature is that, although
Fletcher Norton ran to forty bedrooms, he included only one bathroom.
This seems curious even in an age when most people preferred to take their
bath in front of the fire. One of the mistresses of Grantley Hall, Caroline
Norton, was the grand-daughter of Brindsley Sheridan, the dramatist.

GRASSINGTON

Man has roamed over the Yorkshire Dales from perhaps the dawn of history, and there is an abundance of evidence for the activities of pre-historic man in megaliths such as the Swastika Stone and the Cup and Ring stones near Ilkley, and in earthworks that go back to the Bronze and Iron Ages. A number of very fine artefacts or Romano-British origin have been uncovered in the Settle caves. At Grassington, covering an area of some three hundred acres and spanning a number of public footpaths is a network of stone and turf banks which form the enclosures of a system of fields that reputedly go back to the Second Century A.D. Some of these fields are long and rectangular, measuring as much as 400 feet by 75 feet while others are much smaller and are approximately square. One can also distinguish a number of hut circles and the delineation of narrow roadways defined by banks. Nearby at Lea Green there is an enclosed village site. All this provides evidence of a very well organized system of agriculture at work in the Romano-British period between about 200 and 400 A.D.

Romano-British Field System

HALIFAX 1

Mixenden Old Hall, a small stone manor house overlooking the Ogden
Valley near Halifax, is equipped with both priest-holes and, according to
tradition, also a ghost that used to appear regularly seated on an old
rocking-chair. Nobody knows for certain who the ghost is but there is a
story of a rough, unkempt looking man who appeared at the Hall one
Sunday when the family was at church. The frightened maid-servant let
him in and gave him food, but apparently the exhausted traveller fell
asleep over his victuals with his mouth hanging wide open. Two pistols
stuck through his belt aroused the girl's suspicion that he might be a
highwayman, and, taking the pan of boiling gruel from the fire, she poured
it down his throat. The terribly afflicted highwayman leaped to his feet
but almost immediately collapsed on the floor and died. Possibly the ghost
in the rocking-chair is his, though one feels that it should be that of the
maid-servant stricken with remorse after her cruel action. Mixenden Hall
was probably originally a wooden building that was encased in stone at
about 1600. The owners, the Catholic Illingworths who also owned most
of the Ogden Valley, took the precaution when rebuilding of including
two priest's-holes, each of them little more than cupboards within which a
cramped cleric might conceal himself during an emergency.

Mixenden Old Hall

HALIFAX 2

One of the most interesting buildings in Halifax from the historical and architectural point of view is the famous Piece Hall in Thomas Street. Although the cloth trade dates back to the fifteenth century, this unique quadrangular building was originally opened in 1779 at the beginning of the Industrial Revolution as a marketing hall for the sale of "pieces" of cloth by clothiers from all over Calderdale. The Piece Hall itself, a Georgian building constructed in a series of multi-storey collonades, opening into a large quadrangle or courtyard is in sharp contrast to the formidable Victorian facade with its iron gates, bearing the crest of the old Halifax Corporation, through which one must enter. The building, listed by the Department of the Environment as a building of outstanding architectural interest, has recently been restored to its former impressive splendour and is now open to the public most appropriately as a museum of textile archaeology.

HALIFAX 3

No visitor to Halifax who has an interest in history should miss an opportunity of spending a few hours at Shibden Hall, a fine old fifteenth century, timber-framed house on what used to be the turnpike road from Halifax to Wakefield. Shibden Hall, now open as a folk museum, is handsomely set in spacious parklands with a boating lake and a children's playground. It comprises many features of interest including a fine set of rooms, furnished mostly with seventeenth century furniture: bedrooms; parlour; kitchen; and powder closet, all conveying an excellent impression of the life of the period.

The outbuildings, also, are of particular interest. The Pennine barn, for example, built in 1670 contains a wide variety of agricultural implements of the early nineteenth century as well as a first-rate collection of horse drawn vehicles dating from 1725, including a stage coach and a genuine gipsy caravan.

The craft workshops surrounding the nearby courtyard give a lively impression of ongoing activity, as though wheelwright, blacksmith, and farrier had just knocked off for lunch. The brewhouse, incidentally, came originally from "The Old White Bear" at Norwood Green.

It was at Sibden Hall that Kier Hardie, the Scottish miner who became Member of Parliament for West Ham in 1892 held many meetings around the time of the inception of Independent Labour Party at the end of the Nineteenth Century.

HAMBLETON STREET

Just above Kilburn near the famous White Horse is a spot known as Scotch Corner, and this may well be an important clue to the past, for the wide path that winds up onto the Hambleton Hills and runs north along the edge of the escarpment until it drops through the defile of Scarth Nick by Swainby to cross the A172 is the centuries' old Hambleton Street, sometimes called Hambleton Drove, used by cattle drovers, particularly the Scots, to drive their cattle south. Hambleton Street has been used as a highway from the earliest times, far back beyond the Romans, beyond the Bronze Age, even as far as Neolithic times, as the many tumuli and earthworks such as Hesketh Dike proclaim. No doubt the Scots used it also on their many raids south into Yorkshire, but it is believed to have been simply a part of a great highway that ran from Scotland right down to the Channel, a kind of proto-type Great North Road. South of the Hambleton Hills, Hambleton Street divided, one half passing on through the Plain of York and beyond, and the other going through the Howardian Hills as far as Malton. The driving of cattle south reached its peak in the mid-nineteenth century when not far short of one and a half million sheep and cattle were driven down to Smithfield in one year. In order to negotiate the rough and stony tracks cattle were even fitted with iron shoes specially designed for cloven hoofs and known as "cues".

HARDCASTLE CRAGGS

Not far from the predominantly industrial town of Hebden Bridge lies a rugged, beautiful, yet intractable countryside where formerly communications were very difficult. It is scarcely surprising that in earlier times a people of determined independence of character flourished in this area, and that sometimes independence ran to lawlessness. It was here in the eighteenth century that the coiners of Cragg Vale pursued their unlawful ends, clipping surplus gold from the edges of the King's revenue. Men of apparent respectability and substance were involved in this lucrative but nefarious trade, led by one "King" David Hartley who lived at Bell House in Cragg Vale. Unfortunately for Hartley and his associates the Government had become suspicious. William Dighton, a revenue man of keen perception was sent to Halifax as supervisor of taxes. His vigilance led to Harley's arrest in 1769. Instead of keeping quiet, the coiners waylaid Dighton and murdered him as he walked home from work.

Dighton's murderers were quickly apprehended and brought to justice. Hartley was hanged at York and his body was left suspended in chains on Beacon Hill, later to be buried near the ruins of the Church of St Thomas a' Beckett at Heptonstall. Relics of the coiners can be seen in the local museums, and at The Dusty Miller Inn in Mytholmroyd where a plaque records the coiners' meeting place.

HARDRAW SCAR

Look up at the cascading water of Hardraw Force and you might find it
difficult to believe that the waterfall was given a necessary facial repair
during 1899 after floods had swept great torrents of water down from
Great Shunter Fell and distorted the lip over which the water falls so that
it merely dribbled through mud and shale undramatically. Bridges had been
torn away. Gravestones had been ripped up in the churchyard at Hardraw,
but, when Lord Wharncliffe learned from his estate manager that the
waterfall had been spoilt, he gave his imperious command that all should
be restored without delay. And so it was.

Hardraw Scar was, during the nineteenth century, the traditional site
for a famous outdoor brass band contest which drew bands from all over
Yorkshire and beyond. Beginning in 1880 Besses o' th' Barn, Wike
Temperance, and, best known of all, Black Dyke Mills Band met annually
to compete under the waterfall. During those successful years people
would flock to Hardraw Scar in numbers similar to those attending
modern pop festivals. Unfortunately the contest petered out in 1927
when only two bands competed. However, there is a movement afoot to
revive the old tradition. All strength to its oboes (or, more properly, to its
trombones!)

HAREWOOD HOUSE

John Carr of York rose from humble origins to become one of Yorkshire's most prestigious and distinguished architects as we can see from his prime achievement, Harewood House. By the time Edwin Lascelles commissioned him to build Harewood House he had already built the Grandstand of York Knavesmire and many other fine buildings, though he began as a very humble stone mason. He told a friend that, as a young man he had to stay in bed once while his breeches were patched. As a mason he would leave his home in Horbury on a Monday morning with a large circular meat pie that was to last him for a whole working week, divided equally into six parts.

Harewood House, a solid eighteenth century mansion, has much to offer the visitor, including an Adam interior and much fine furniture by that other master craftsman of Yorkshire, Thomas Chippendale. Indeed, it was the Earl of Harewood who noticed Chippendale and became his patron. There is also a bird garden and extensive grounds all originally designed and laid out by that indefatigable landscaping genius Capability Brown.

HARROGATE

Like most large holiday centres Harrogate is a mixture of that which is repulsive and of that which is attractive. Many of its buildings, including the vast and pompous Royal Baths Assembly Rooms, built in the 1870s, demonstrate the worst vices of Victorian architecture. The Royal Pump Room Museum itself is scarcely to be classed as one of the most beautiful of buildings, yet it stands above the original sulphur well in Crescent Road. For all this, however, Harrogate is the leading spa in the North of England, and an exceedingly pleasant location in which to stay, especially for the valitudinarian, having as it does no fewer than eighty-eight springs of both sulphurous and chalybeate waters. Because of its comparative propinquity to the Dales and historical sites of all kinds, it has developed into a thriving holiday centre containing a variety of excellent shops. It is also a focus for the antique trade and The North Antique Dealers' Fair is held there annually in September.

The middle of the town is almost completely encircled by a vernal area consisting of two hundred acres of lawns fringed by trees. Situated on the Stray, as this belt is called, is the Tewit Well, oldest of all the medicinal springs in the town. It was here that William Slingsby noticed the excellent quality of the waters as early as 1571, and it is perhaps largely to him that Harrogate owes its thanks for its present prosperity.

HAWORTH

Here at the top of Haworth main street on the edge of the grim high
presence of Haworth Moor we feel ourselves in the Bronte country.

The grey, unpretentious parsonage, now the Bronte Museum, seems still
to harbour its secrets of desperate genius striving to express itself amidst
isolation, poverty, and frail health. By 1822 the Bronte family was
motherless, six small children and their Irish father, the Rev Patrick
Bronte. Two of the girls died very young at a boarding school for the
daughters of clergymen, later roundly condemned as the Lowood of "Jane
Eyre", and the others, Charlotte, Patrick Branwell, Emily, and Anne lived
on, frequently lonely and always frustrated and intensely unhappy.

For Patrick Branwell unhappiness proved too heavy a burden. He
became the centre of bitter wrangling and contention within the family.
He drank heavily at "The Black Bull Inn", took opium, and died of
consumption.

For the sisters, fortunately, another channel of release was open: all
three had been born with a measure of literary ability. No book in English
literature expresses the tempestuous power of thwarted passion better
than Emily's "Wuthering Heights", and, perhaps, no book makes a better
plea for the fullness of life than Charlotte's "Jane Eyre".

By 1855 all the children of Patrick Bronte were dead, none of them
having survived until the age of forty, while he was left to brood on alone
for a few more years at the parsonage.

HELMSLEY

Recorded in the Domesday Book at Elmeslac, the attractive town of
Helmsley stands beside the River Rye on the edge of the magnificent
North Yorkshire Moors National Park, an area of most outstanding beauty.
It is excellently situated as a jumping off point for visits to a number of
historical sites, including the Abbeys of Rievaulx and Byland, and
Pickering Castle.

In Plantagenet times and for many years afterwards there was a castle at
Helmsley but today all that remains, under the devoted care of the
Ministry of Works, is a ruined barbican and gatehouse. The most active
period in the life of Helmsley Castle was during the Civil War when Sir
Thomas Fairfax laid siege to it in 1644. Sir John Crosland held it in the
name of the King for three months before surrendering in November.

In the vast market place of Helmsley stands the Black Swan Hotel,
incorporating the Georgian houses and a much older building, as the
substantial ceiling timbers show. In times past The Black Swan did sterling
service as a coaching inn.

HEPTONSTALL

Standing high and looking across a magnificent stretch of moorland
Heptonstall is the oldest and perhaps the most beautiful village in West
Yorkshire. Along its winding, narrow streets crowd old weavers' cottages
and interesting stone-built houses with fascinating gateways and ginnels.

The ruins of the thirteenth century church of St. Thomas à Beckett
stand picturesquely within the churchyard of the present parish church, a
fine nineteenth century building. Here "King" David Hartley, the leader of
the coiners of Cragg Vale lies buried. Here also is the seventeenth century
Grammar School, now a museum where one can see some of the original
school desks still preserved long after the pupils who lolled behind them
over their Latin primers have been laid to rest.

Heptonstall is now a well-known centre of art and craft, attracting
annually many artists and lovers of scenic beauty.

Long Causeway, a medieval packhorse road, runs from the village over
the hills to Burnley.

HIGH ELDWICK

On the edge of Rombalds Moor nestles the old "Fleece Inn", better known by everybody to whom Yorkshire is familiar as "Dick Hudson's". The old inn, strategically placed close to the old packhorse route that runs up from Bingley to Ilkley, was at the very spot to attract the crowds of textile workers from the mills in Bradford and Bingley as they poured forth, especially during Easter weekends in the nineteenth century. It became almost a matter of tradition for mill-workers, seeking fresh air and an hour or two of liberty to trek in large numbers over Rombalds Moor towards Ilkley, the most hardy, perhaps, reaching as far as Ilkley and back in one day. Dick Hudson's made a convenient stopping place for roast beef and Yorkshire pudding at a shilling per head, or perhaps a ploughman's lunch for a couple of pennies. The "Fleece Inn" became the property of Thomas Hudson in 1809. Dick, his son, who gave the establishment its name, took over in 1850 and kept the place going until he died in 1878. This was "Dick Hudson's" heyday. They planned to put in pleasure gardens and other amenities towards the end of Queen Victoria's reign but instead the inn was demolished and replaced by the present building in 1900. The textile workers may not now flock in their thousands over Rombald's Moor but the visitor can still enjoy visiting the site of their roisterous Easter meals.

Dick Hudson's

HUBBERHOLME

Hubberholme, twenty-one miles from Skipton and in the neck of
Langstrothdale is a village well worth a visit. Extremely small, compact
and cosy in summer, it is a village in which there are more sheep than
humans. Its church and inn have an interesting and connected history;
until comparatively recently they were joined within the same benefice.
The church, originally established in 1241 by William de Percy and now
dedicated to Saint Michael and All Angels, has passed through the spiritual
hands also of Saint Oswald and Saint Leonard. It has at least once been
flooded so that fish swam between the pews. New pews have more
recently been installed by Robert Thompson, the "mouse-man" wood
carver of Kilburn and his signature in the form of carved mice is noticed
by the observant visitor. Other events in the history of Hubberholme are
recorded in stained glass for an excellent new window was completed in
1970 by John Skeat. This window depicts among other things the
carpenter William Jake at work restoring the rood loft in the sixteenth
century and Thomas Lindley of Hulton Gill who, many a Sunday in the
early years of the nineteenth century rode over to take services at Hubberholme. Talking of horsemanship, another cleric, the Archdeacon Boyd
caused a stone cross to be raised above the east end in thanks to God for
his narrow escape when his horse bolted at Starbotton.

HULL ARCHAEOLOGICAL MUSEUM

Hull can boast an almost unique collection of Roman mosaics of the Constantian Period, circa 306 to 361. A.D. In the nineteen-thirties excavations were carried out on the site of two Roman buildings at Rudston. Both yielded magnificent finds in the form of mosaic floors. The smaller house, an L shaped building contained several, chief among them The Charioteer Mosaic, now to be seen along with all the others in the Archaeological Museum.

The so-called "Charioteer Mosaic" is, in fact, a large panel measuring fifteen feet, nine inches by thirteen feet, nine inches, the centre circle being occupied by the representation of a triumphant charioteer. In his left hand he bears the palm frond of victory, while, in his right, held proudly aloft, he flaunts the wreath that is to be his crown. His head is covered by protective headgear. On his body he wears the tightly laced corselage that is designed to protect his rib cage. The red tunic proclaims him to be a member of the "red club'. or "the red devils", no doubt aces among charioteers.

Other mosaics in the collection include the smaller "Leopards' Panel" and the particularly impressive "Venus Mosaic", a highly imaginative representation of the Goddess of Love with a Triton or Merman in attendance, bearing in his hand a flaming torch.

HULL 1

A cursory glance at St Nicholas's, West Hull might incline the visitor to believe that he was looking at a late medieval church, though one of surprisingly individual character. This is because St Nicholas's was built by the twentieth century architect, Dr John Bilston. Bilston can scarcely be shrugged off as a mere neo-gothic. His work has a character and individuality that seems to be distilled from the essence of the man himself. He was a person of rare intellectual capacity, a classical scholar with interests in every branch of the arts from architecture to music, as well as a phenomenal capacity for work of the highest order. It is characteristic of his integrity and a tribute to his deep religious devotion that, when the tower of St Nicholas's was threatened, not because of an error in design but because of an unknown geological fault, he had it rebuilt on new foundations entirely at his own expense.

In 1930, when he was seventy four, instead of retiring, Dr John turned his mind to a new enquiry, that of medieval town planning. This study resulted in some quite remarkable findings on Hull as it was in 1293. Wyke-on-Hull as it was then called was already a seaport of considerable importance.

St Nicholas's Church

HULL 2

Kingston-upon-Hull, or Hull as it is usually called, is justly proud of its
most distinguished philanthropist, William Wilberforce. He was born in
1759 in the Jacobean house now preserved as a museum in the High
Street, the son of a merchant of the town. Until Wilberforce joined the
evangelical sect nicknamed by Sidney Smith "The Clapham Sect", his
dissolute style of life gave little hint of what was to follow, but from that
time he threw himself into humanitarian work of all kinds with unceasing
energy. As an M.P. for Yorkshire, and making the fullest use of his lifelong
friendship with William Pitt, he adopted the cause of slavery as his greatest
focus of concern. It was a hard and bitter struggle as many of the members
of parliament had interests in the slave trade, and even Pitt, though
opposed to slavery in principle, was not prepared to place his parliamentary career at risk. In 1807, however, with Fox's help, an act was
passed forbidding the slave trade in British dominions. The crowning
achievement, the abolition of slavery within British dominions, came in
1833, and Wilberforce received news of his triumph as he lay on his death
bed.

The museum contains personal mementoes of Wilberforce and items of
local history as well as rooms furnished in the styles of various periods.
Wilberforce's humanitarianism is also marked by the Wilberforce
monument, standing over one hundred feet high before the College of
Technology in Lowgate.

Wilberforce House

HULL 3

Should the visitor to Hull be in the vicinity of Silver Street at about noon, it is likely that he will seek to refresh himself in "Ye Olde White Harte Inn". As he sits in the oak-panelled luncheon room, piquancy may be lent to his appetite by the knowledge that the room he is sitting in is also known as "The Plotting Room" for it was here in 1642 that the elders of the city under the chairmanship of the owner of this house, the military governor, Sir John Hotham, decided to refuse admittance within the city gates to King Charles I. On April 23rd, 1642 the King sent a messenger announcing that he was on his way from York and that he wished to dine with Sir John. As a result of the meeting in "The Plotting Room" the King was turned back from the "Beverley Gate" (demolished in 1776). At five o'clock the King sent a Herald into the city to ask if Sir John had changed his mind, and receiving a further refusal, he declared Sir John a traitor and returned to York.

This was not the end of the matter, for later the Parliamentary side became suspicious that Sir John and his son had changed their allegiance and planned to surrender the city to the Royalists after all. During a dramatic attempt to escape and reach his house in the village of Scarborough, nine miles away, Sir John was captured and committed to the Tower. In 1645, after languishing in jail for three years, both Sir John and his son, Captain Hotham, were tried and beheaded.

Such are the fortunes of war!

Ye Olde White Harte Inn

HUMBER KEEL

During the Middle Ages an important but erratic link between Doncaster and Sheffield was the River Don. When the need for reliable communication became more pressing at the beginning of the eighteenth century, steps were taken to render the Don permanently navigable all the year round between the two cities.

In the heyday of the South Yorkshire Navigation, the craft most frequently seen on the river was the Humber Keel, a large, blunt-nosed barge with a single square sail. The Humber Keel could be either sailed or hauled by men. In 1762, however, the right hand bank of the river, going upstream, was adapted to accommodate companies of heavy horses to pull the barges.

At about 1880 most of the old Humber keels began to disappear in favour of steam-powered barges, while in the early 1900s short squat barges pulled in trains and known as 'Tom Puddings' were introduced to provide fuel for the power stations. These, in their turn began to be supplanted in the 1930s by motor barges, while, as late as 1971 push-towing of barge trains was brought in.

Like the canals, "The Navigation" was threatened in the 1840s by the introduction of the railways and was taken over by the South Yorkshire Railway with detrimental results. Little work was done on maintenance and no encouragement was given to traffic. However, with the transfer of stock to the Sheffield and South Yorkshire Navigation Co matters improved again and today "The Navigation" provides both benefit and enjoyment to those who use it.

ILKLEY

In the heart of Wharfedale and surrounded by lonely and impressive
moorlands lies the spa town of Ilkley. It was in the mid-nineteenth
century, when wealthy Victorians came in search of the supposedly
health-giving waters that the great boom in Ilkley's prosperity began. Since
about 1842 it has enjoyed increasing prestige, and, between the two world
wars, many wool merchants found it an agreeable area in which to set up
their "baronial" homes.

The real historical interest of Ilkley lies in its proximity to the moors
where there is an abundance of megalithic stones to give signposts to the
remote past. The most famous of those are the Cup and Ring Rock at
Green Crag Slack and the Swastika Stone near the head of Hebers Gill.
Nobody is certain of the origin or purpose of these stones which are
thought to date from the Early Iron Age.

Mystery also surrounds the origin of the well-known anthem "On Ilkla'
Moor Baht'at" which goes back to at least the eighteen sixties. Nobody
knows for sure who wrote the words but they are often attributed to a
Sutton man named Fenegan.

In recent years the ecological character of Ilkley Moor has changed
owing to the depredations of sheep and the alarming spread of crowberry
at the expense of heather, but steps are now being taken to reduce over-
grazing.

Cup and Ring Rock

DURHAM.-
MIDDLESBOROUGH
THORNABY
STOKE
WESTMORLAND.
BARNARD CASTLE
BOWES.
RICHMOND
CATTERICK.
MUKER
O SMOTHERLEY
N. ALLERTON
SEDBURG
HARDROW
HAWES
ASKRIGG
LEYBURN
BEDALE
DENT
WENSLEY
SNAPE
JERVAULX ABBEY
KILBUR
COX
MASHAM
TOPCLIFFE
BUCKDEN
EASING
INGLETON
CHAPEL LE DALE
HORTON IN RIBBLESDALE.
HIGH BENTHAM
AUSTWICK
CLAPHAM
STAINFORTH
KILNSEY
FOUNTAINS ABBEY
RIPON
NEWBY HALL
BOROUGHBRIDGE
GIGGLESWICK
JETTLE
GRASSINGTON
MALHAM
PATELEY BR
ALDBOROUGH.-
BURNSALL
RIPLEY
SLAIDBURN
SKIPTON
BOLTON ABBEY
HARROWGATE
BARNOLDSWICK
EARBY
OTLEY
WETHERBY
KEIGHLEY
TADCASTER
ELDWICK
TAWTON
HAWORTH
BINGLEY
SHIPLEY
KIRKSTALL ABBEY
SHERE
BRADFORD
LEEDS
OLEDSH
QUEENSBURY -
HEPTONSTALL
HEBDEN BR.
SOWERBY BR
BIRSTALL.
CASTLEFORD
HALIFAX
BRIGHOUSE
KNOTTIN
DEWSBURY
WAKEFIELD
LANCASHIRE
HUDDERSFIELD
BADSWORTH
SLAITHWAITE
HOLMFIRTH
CAWTHORNE
BARNSLEY
PENISTONE
WORSBOROUGH
W
MEXBOROUGH
WENTWORTH
CO
CHESHIRE
ROTHERHAM
M
SHEFFIELD
DERBYSHIRE

64

REDCAR
SALTBURN
LOFTUS
HINDERWELL
GUISBOROUGH
GLAISDALE
WHITBY
ETON
DANBY
OUGHTON
EGTON
HAWSKER
GROSMONT
ROBIN HOOD'S BAY
HOPGATE
RAVENSCAR
ILSDALE
CLOUGTON
ROSEDALE
WHEELDALE MOOR.
SCARBOROUGH
LAND
AYTON
KIRBY MOORSIDE
PICKERING
WYKEHAM
IEVAUX ABBEY
THORNTON
HELMSLEY
LE DALE.
FILEY
AMPLEFORTH
HOVINGHAM
NORTON
WINTRINGHAM
MALTON
WEAVERTHORPE
FLAMBOROUGH
HEAD.
STLE HOWARD
N. GRIMSTON
RUDSTON
BRIDLINGTON
SLEDMERE
LANGTOFT
BURTON AGNES
KIRKHAM
ABBEY
BARMSTON
FRIDAYTHORPE
GT DRIFFIELD
STAMFORD BR
HUGGATE
SKIPSEA
YORK
KEXBY
MILLINGTON
ATWICK
WARTER
MIDDLETON
HORNSEA
MARKET WEIGHTON
RICCALL
BISHOPBURTON
BEVERLEY
OSGODBY
SELBY
SKIDBY
HOWDEN
BROUGH
WITHERNSEA
HESSLE
HULL
GOOLE
R. HUMBER.
SUNK
ISLAND
EASINGTON
KILNSEA
THORNE
LINCOLNSHIRE
SPURN POINT
HATFIELD
DONCASTER
BAWTRY
NORTH SEA.

IVELET

If you are a connoisseur of bridges, especially hump-back bridges, go to Ivelet in Swaledale where there exists what is, perhaps, the most hump-backed bridge of them all. It was built about three hundred years ago to accommodate the packhorses on the bridle way to Muker, probably by workers who had newly immigrated from Stranraer in Scotland. The bridge is eight feet, three inches wide, and its twenty-five foot high arch was originally constructed in a wooden frame. Nobody can say why the arch was built so high, but, whether by design of accident, it has served the bridge well. The newer bridge built at Gunnerside in the nineteenth century to take the diverted main road was in many ways less successful. In the last century it was washed away no fewer than three times.

A stone beside Ivelet Bridge closely resembling a coffin, and in fact known locally as "the Coffin Stone" gives rise to macabre speculation though, in fact, it was placed there in comparatively recent years probably to reinforce the bridge. Nevertheless Ivelet Bridge has had its share of ghostly visitations, including ladies in black and a donkey with brass eyes. No doubt most of these alleged hauntings date back to the old lead-mining days and are to be associated less with the world of supernatural spirits than with the more earthly spirits with which the miners regaled themselves on a Saturday night!

Ivelet Bridge

JERVAULX ABBEY

Of all the abbey remains in Yorkshire perhaps Jervaulx appeals most strangely to the sense of mystery and romance. Established in 1156 by the Cistercians and named after the River Ure (or Yere) beside which it stands, Jervaulx exercised a considerable influence, particularly in Wensleydale and Ribblesdale, for four centuries. The monks became famous as sheep breeders and horse rearers. The horses of Jervaulx were well-respected as a separate breed, most of them being reared in the Horton-in-Ribblesdale area as the name Studford near Horton suggests. It is probable that the monks of Jervaulx were also responsible for that most edible of products Wensleydale cheese.

Though Prior Aylmer in Walter Scott's "Ivanhoe" is a particularly jovial prior, Jervaulx was not free from sadness and bloodshed. The last abbot, Abbot Sedbar, became involved somewhat reluctantly in the Pilgrimage of Grace for which he was hanged at Tyburn in 1547. After the Dissolution the roodscreen was secretly conveyed to Aysgarth Church and Jervaulx was left a decaying ruin for centuries. Many of its squared stones were removed for building work elsewhere, though the builders rejected curved stones that were unsuitable for their purpose. The Earl of Ailesbury put a firm stop to this plundering in 1805, and since then the Abbey ruins have been in the hands of people who care to preserve them in a state of dignity befitting their noble past.

KEIGHLEY AND WORTH VALLEY RAILWAY

Yorkshire has a great deal to offer those who are interested in the development of the railway.

The Keighley and Worth Valley Railway, running between Keighley, through Haworth, to Oxenhope gives one a glimpse into a past when locomotives steamed through the countryside like personable dinosaurs. The line, operated now by volunteer enthusiasts, and having a varied collection of over thirty locomotives, first opened in 1867 at the height of the age of "Railway Mania". It runs a daily service through the summer months, and, throughout the year there are services at weekends and on bank holidays.

In York, appropriately, in the National Railway Museum, housed in an old British Railways steam locomotive shed are twenty-five historic locomotives, including "The Flying Scotsman", "Mallard", "Henry Oakley", and "Evening Star" together with a number of decorated royal coaches.

The man who perhaps did more than anyone else to promote the railway system in Britain was George Hudson, a linen draper of York. In 1835 he promoted his first railway, The York and North Midland. By 1848 he controlled between a half and one third of the 5000 miles of track operating in Britain. Unfortunately his business methods were very much open to question and he was discredited. However, at his death, Gladstone, who had been his chief opponent, said of him: "No mere speculator, but a projector of great discernment, courage, and rich enterprise".

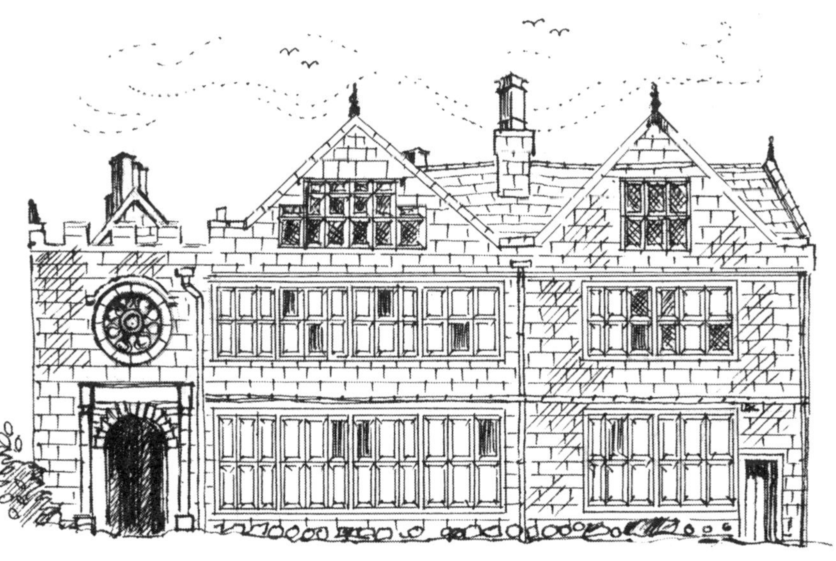

KEIGHLEY

Keighley is a town with a short history, having grown up in the last
century during a boom in the textile trade when cottons and worsteds
became suddenly important and profitable, but it contains one historical
building of a very fine order, the late seventeenth century manor house of
East Riddlesden Hall, now owned by the National Trust. The Hall itself
contains much excellent panelling, which is seen to good advantage in the
principal bedroom, and also some fine plasterwork. It has a great
banqueting hall and is most tastefully furnished in the fashion of the
period like most properties that are in the care of the National Trust. For
example, the flagstoned kitchen, beautifully laid out with logs in the
fireplace, an inviting wooden settle, a spinning wheel, and an excellent
collection of pewter plates, tankards, jugs, etc, appears to be waiting for
the return of its amiable seventeenth century ghosts.

Out in the grounds there is a fishpond and two barns, one of which,
many years older than the house itself, is considered to be one of the
finest tithe barns in the North of England.

KILBURN

Cut into the side of the hill beside the village of Kilburn, six miles east of
Thirsk, is the great White Horse. Some 314 feet long and 228 feet high,
and visible on a clear day, it is claimed, from as far away as Harrogate and
Leeds, the White Horse was the brainchild of one, John Hodgson, a local
schoolmaster who with the help of his pupils completed it in 1857 no
doubt in pursuit of laudible scholastic ends.

Less spectacular but of infinitely more interest to those who appreciate
craftsmanship is the work of the "Mouse Man" of Kilburn, the master
woodcarver Robert Thompson who "signed" all his work with the figure
of a mouse. Although Thompson died in 1955, his workshop next to
"The Foresters' Arms" continues to keep his craft alive, for this is the
major industry of Kilburn. Examples of Robert Thompson's superb work
are to be found in the local church.

A strange and obscure tradition preserved in Kilburn is the Kilburn
"Feast" held in July. After sports, children's games, and numerous
examples of high jollification, "The Lord Mayor of Kilburn" accompanied
by "The Lady Mayoress", really a young man in disguise, go from house to
house imposing fines on the villagers for all sorts of imaginary offences.

KILNSEY

Kilnsey Crag, with its forbidding and "unclimbable" overhang dominates the Wharfedale Road from above the village of Kilnsey to such an extent that visitors are often challenged to throw a penny in the hope that they may hit the Crag from the road. The summit itself provides the focus annually for a curious contest that is definitely not for those who are short of breath or weak in limb. At Kilnsey's Annual Show fell runners race to the top and back trying to break the astonishing record time of eight minutes, nineteen seconds! The village of Kilnsey was for several generations the seat of the Wade family, and it was Christopher Wade who built Kilnsey Old Hall in 1648, surprisingly perhaps since the Civil War was on. Though the War apparently left the people of Upper Wharfedale comparatively undisturbed, Christopher's son, Cuthbert, was, in fact, captured while fighting on the Royalist side, and released only after paying a ransom amounting to one sixth of his assets. Cuthbert subsequently joined his father at Kilnsey Old Hall and lived there as its host after his father's death. At one time he had the doubtful privilege of entertaining Lady Anne Clifford of Barden Tower as she was on her way north to visit certain of her properties. The visit, which was repeated as Lady Anne returned the same way, must have cost Cuthbert a small fortune for Lady Anne, though a great benefactress also liked to spend unstintingly and expected to be entertained on a lavish scale.

Kilnsey Hall

KIRKSTALL ABBEY

This picturesque but sad ruin on the outskirts of Leeds is the best
preserved Cistercian Abbey in the country. Indeed, so much remains of its
former beauty that, in the nineteenth century a strong but regrettably
ineffective attempt was made to have it fully restored, and Gilbert Scott,
the architect responsible for the Neo-Gothic Anglican Cathedral in
Liverpool, was called in as a consultant.

The Cistercians arrived at the Kirkstall Abbey site in the year 1152,
thirteen monks and ten lay brothers, having decided to colonize because they
considered the land thereabouts suitable for cultivation. However, the
Cistercians were by no means first in the field for the place was already
occupied by a community of hermits under the direction of one Seleth, a
contemplative who had received his vocation in a vision. It is not clear
what agreement the Cistercians reached with the followers of Seleth during
this monastic take-over, though it is known that a number of them joined
the Cistercian order.

The community lived in a state of robust health until the time of the
Dissolution, though they were severely reduced by the Black Death in
1349.

The Gatehouse, a substantial building of character in its own right, now
serves as a folk museum.

KNARESBOROUGH 1

The very picturesque town of Knaresborough with its Georgian houses winds down in steep slopes and a series of alleyways to the River Nidd whose gorge it dominates.

Many historical events can be recalled here. For example, it was in the medieval court of Knaresborough at the entrance to the Castle that the three murderers of Thomas à Beckett, fearful of the terrible vengeance of the King sought refuge and hid for three years in terror. It was here also that the ill-fated King Richard II was imprisoned on his way to an ignominious death at Pontefract.

Between here and York at Marston Moor one of the two great battles of the Civil War raged. Prince Rupert, nephew of Charles I, led his troops to meet what he considered to be a band of rabble led by Oliver Cromwell, clashing with them on the Moor July 2nd, 1644. This proved to be the turning point of the war, for Cromwell, having recruited an army of stalwart farmers' sons, had trained and drilled them to a point where they were more than a match for the King's army. This famous defeat opened the way to the decisive Battle of Naseby fought in 1645. Weapons and armour used in the Battle of Marston Moor can be seen in the museum at Knaresborough.

More modestly, perhaps, stands The Castle Mill, built in 1785, the oldest linen mill in England.

Here also "Blind Jack of Knaresborough" was born, road builder and bridge builder before the days of Telford and Macadam.

Above all this, with an impressive view over the town, stands The Castle and the implacable keep of John of Gaunt

KNARESBOROUGH 2

Mother Shipton, the weird old seer of Knaresborough, was born on the site of the cave circa July 1488. A woman of rare persuasiveness, she managed to convince her contemporaries and many since that she could look far into the future. Many of her forecasts have indeed been realized. For example, she foretold the development of aircraft. Whether she worked through imagination, divination, or pure fabrication we may shortly have the opportunity of discovering for, in the words of her last forecast:

"The world then to an end shall come

In Nineteen Hundred and Eighty-one."

Mother Shipson's cave was first exhibited in the reign of Charles I.

Nearby is the so-called "Dropping-Well" where water drops from an overhang, leaving a deposit of calcium carbonate on any interposed object. Visitors have hung purses, shoes, hats, and other porous objects under the dropping water since the well was first opened to the public in 1630. It is estimated that some 700 gallons of water flows per day over the face of the rock.

An eerie collection of objects can be seen in various stages of petrification, including two excrescences that began as hats in 1853.

The Dropping Well

LEDSHAM

It is hard to believe that such a delightful and unspoilt village as Ledsham should exist with its mellow limestone walls so close to such an intensely industrial area as Castleford. Some have claimed that Ledsham Church is one of the oldest ecclesiastical sites in Yorkshire and there is, indeed, evidence of Saxon work. The present church, founded by Robert de Lacy retains a number of Norman features. Inside there is a curious monument to Lady Bolles, the daughter of William Witham of nearby Ledston Hall, who is said to have died of witchcraft in 1593, the black spells that led to her death having been cast by a certain Mary Pannel. Mary Pannel and her malevolent powers must have been taken very seriously by the people of the area since there is a hill named after her on a section of Roman road that runs from Castleford to Aberford about a mile and a half to the West of Ledsham.

The residents of Ledston Hall were generally philanthropic, and Lady Betty Hastings, who worshipped in Ledsham church was well-known for her good works. She founded the charity school that stands next to the church and, among other acts of benevolence, donated her properties at Wheldale to provide scholarships at Queen's College, Oxford.

The Village Church

LEEDS

What solid, terrifying pride in present achievement and future expectation is expressed by the monumental neo-classical presence of Leeds Town Hall, designed by Cuthbert Brodrick in 1853! The confidence of those Victorian gentlemen basking in the sunshine of Prince Albert's Great Exhibition was not altogether unwarranted as we can see from the modern city which has dubbed itself "The Capital of the Centre of Britain", for the industrial and civic achievements of Leeds have been almost unrivalled.

There are, however, other faces of Leeds which will be of interest to the visitor in the search of history. The Leeds Playhouse, for example, with its thrust stage from where the BBC presents its programme "The Good Old Days", is reported to be the last surviving musical hall in England, a living memento of the age of Marie Lloyd and Sir Harry Lauder in which audience participation was more than a myth.

In the Borough of Pudsey, in 1746, largely through the work of an Ossett man, Benjamin Ingham, a flourishing Moravian settlement was established. Ingham, like Wesley originally an Anglican clergyman, had caused some offence within the Church because of his unorthodox preaching methods and his propensity for addressing the faithful in outhouses, in dilapidated barns as well as in the open air. The Moravians had a strong link with the Methodists for it was with this Georgian protestant sect that Wesley had spent two very formative years between 1736 and 1738.

We cannot leave Pudsey without recalling its outstanding contribution to the national game of cricket, for it was from Pudsey that the great Yorkshire and England batsman Sir Leonard Hutton came.

The Town Hall

MALHAM COVE

Malham Cove with its nine hundred feet long cliff rising to three hundred feet above Malham Beck is a truly impressive and spectacular sight for the visitor and it must have struck Charles Kingsley forcibly when he visited it in 1858 seeking material for a book he intended to write on the Pilgrimage of Grace, for the book on the Pilgrimage of Grace was never written but five years later he wrote "The Water Babies". The words "at the foot of a limestone crag the great fountain rose" are almost certainly inspired by Malham Cove, and his description of the area must be based upon the notes he made when as he visited the Craven millionaire Walter Morrison at Tarn House. The river that poor Tom drowned in was almost certainly the Skirfare a short distance to the north. Tarn House, left to the National Trust by Walter Morrison when he died, is now a field centre. Malham Cove is about three quarters of a mile from Malham Village which was founded in about 600 A.D. by the Angles. Through the village runs the Pennine Way, the longest footpath in Britain; beginning at Edal in Derbyshire and finishing at Kirk Yetholm on the Scottish Border, it is two hundred and fifty miles long.

MALTBY

On a rocky site one and a half miles east of Maltby lie the ruins of the
Abbey of St. Mary of Roche, founded in 1147 by two Norman barons,
Richard de Busli and Richard fitzTurgis. Roche, named after the rocks on
which it was built, was one of the smaller of the Cistercian abbeys that
proliferated throughout Yorkshire in the twelfth century, Rievaulx in
1132, and Fountains Abbey in 1135 being the principal houses.

The Cistercian order was initially a reformed and more austere type of
Benedictinism, which cut out all superfluity of dress and deliberately chose
the loneliest and most barren places for its houses. Quickly, however, the
monks learned the principles of estate management and became adept at
the art of sheep breeding in lonely and normally unproductive areas. They
laid the foundations of Yorkshire's prosperity in wool. Fountains Abbey,
for example, at the height of its power managed estates in one hundred and
fifty one parishes throughout the Country. The monks were, however, in
danger of becoming too worldly, and this was one of Henry VIII's
principal excuses for the suppression of the monasteries in the sixteenth
century. In 1538, at the time of its suppression, Roche was valued at £224
2s 5d, scarcely what one would call a lordly sum even for those days.

A point worth noting is that in 1770 the site of Roche was landscaped
by Capability Brown as part of the Earl of Scarborough's estate.

Roche Abbey

Ilton Stonehenge

MASHAM

In the eighteenth century when it had become the fashion for the rich to employ improvers to landscape their property, many great landowners went a stage further and had a folly or several follies erected on their estates. Most such follies, with which Yorkshire in particular abounds, as their name implies, had little other than decorative value and merely reflected the tastier whims of their inspirers.

Perhaps the strangest of Yorkshire's follies is the Ilton Stonehenge, an imitation Druid's circle erected on the moors near Masham. William Danby's stone circle, or to be more precise William Danby's stone ellipse, was built in about 1820, and, although it has all the elements of a folly, it has been suggested that it may have been erected to express very specific religious or mystical leanings on that gentleman's part. Whatever the truth, the area of the circle is indeed pervaded by a strange preternatural atmosphere quite in keeping with the subject.

A large, rough-stone pillar stands brooding a little apart like a silent and faceless guardian. In a small cave at one end of the ellipse there grows an abundance of a rare species of luminous lichen.

Danby, by all accounts a man of great wealth, is said to have employed his labour force upon the building of the stone ellipse at a time when they would have been otherwise unemployed. The men who laboured away at this imposing edifice, and who were no doubt glad to do so, were paid the noble sum of one shilling a day for their services.

MIDDLETON

The ornate Viking cross in the church of Middleton and dating back to the tenth century A.D. is tangible evidence of the Viking presence in the Danelaw, the area to the north and east of a line running from London to Chester, from the year 793 when, as the Anglo-Saxon Chronicle reports, "Terrible portends appeared over Northumbria, and a little while after that the harrying of the heathen miserably destroyed God's church in Lindisfarne."

The Vikings, named probably after their Viks or coastal creeks, continued to bring war and rapine into England until the Norman Conquest. Even Alfred the Great was forced to come to terms with them, and Ethelred the Unready stupidly paid them Danegold to go away. Predictably they accepted the gold and stayed.

However, as the cross of Middleton declares, many had submitted to the influence of their hosts sufficiently to become Christianized. The cross, a finely wrought object in stone, depicts a Viking warrior laid in his grave. As befits a man of war, he wears his helmet and armour. Beside him on his left rests his sword and his battle-axe, whilst to his right is his long spear. Thus, presumably he awaits the last trump.

Viking Cross

80

NEWBY HALL

Newby Hall, one of Yorkshire's great stately homes, stands beside the River Ure between Ripon and Boroughbridge within twenty-five acres of beautiful gardens. The house, originally built in 1695, was extended and remoulded by Robert Adam during the eighteenth century, and is generally regarded as an Adam masterpiece.

Robert Adam, 1728-1792, as well as being an architect of genius, influenced the making and design of furniture as well as that of buildings. His work is characterized by inlaid decorative motives in which wreaths, fans and the honeysuckle predominate. The best of his wrought-iron work possesses the fineness of filigree. Of particular note are his beautiful ceilings of which the Library of Newby is a striking example, and his fireplaces and mantelpieces which all bear his unmistakable hallmark.

Newby Hall contains many treasures well worth seeing, including the world famous Gobelin Tapestries, some excellent examples of both Greek and Roman sculpture, and much fine Chippendale furniture.

NORTHALLERTON

Lying in the Vale of Mowbray, Northallerton has been called "the Capital of North Yorkshire".

One of the best described events in its history is an account written in the twelth century by Aelred, Abbot of the Cistercian Abbey of Rievaulx of "The Battle of the Standards" fought just to the north of the town. The battle between the Scots and the English occurred on 22nd October, 1138 in the perturbed reign of King Stephen. The Scots, having invaded England, were sweeping aside all resistance and laying waste the countryside in a most barbarous manner. In one of the more felicitous interventions by the Church in worldly matters, the Archibishop of York took upon himself the responsibility of organizing resistance. The focus of his campaign was a tall ship's mast carried on a waggon and bearing a pyx containing the consecrated host. With this the banners of St. Peter of York, St John of Beverley, and St Wilfried of Ripon were erected in a gesture of faith in victory on Cowton Moor. The determination of the prelate was amply justified for the Scots were routed in the battle and put to flight.

Truck House

NORTON CONYERS

This very fine miniature mansion quite close to Ripon has for four
centuries been the family seat of the Graham family. Originally built in the
fourteenth century by Sir Richard Norton, and rebuilt by the Norton
family in the sixteenth century, the house was lost to the Nortons when
Sir Christopher Norton had been given the responsibility of guarding Mary
Queen of Scots while she was imprisoned in Bolton Castle. Mary's charm
prevailed upon her jailer and he joined the Earl of Northumberland in the
abortive Rising of the North in 1569. For this treason, Elizabeth deprived
Sir Christopher of both his property and his life. Through a marriage
between Catherine Musgrave and Sir Richard Graham in 1624 the house
came into the possession of the Grahams who, though thoroughly respect-
able by the seventeenth century, had not long before spent most of their
time cattle rustling and horse stealing along the Scottish border.

Norton Cayners is particularly interesting inside, its Great Hall
containing many fine relics of the past. One room in the house has an
interesting mystery to it, for it is called "Mad Molly's room". Nobody is
quite sure who "Mad Molly" was, though probably she was an
unfortunately deranged member of the family who was incarcerated in the
attic. This cruel fact must have fired Charlotte Bronte's imagination. She
visited the house, probably in 1840 while she was serving as governess to
the Bensons of Swarcliffe. Thus Norton Conyers became the prototype for
what is possibly an even more noble mansion, the Thornfield Hall of "Jane
Eyre".

OSMOTHERLEY

The village of Osmotherley, situated within the North Yorkshire Moors National Park was well beloved by John Wesley who visited it on no fewer than fifteen occasions from 1745 until 1784 when he was eighty-one years old. The story of his first visit is a strangely moving one. Father Peter Adams, a Franciscan, having been as impressed by the preaching of Wesley, persuaded him to go and preach in Osmotherley. Wesley came from Northallerton and arrived in the village shortly before midnight on April 15th, 1745, when he immediately began to preach with great effect. On the following morning at the early hour of five a.m. he preached again to a large congregation, many of whom had stayed up all night in order not to miss him.

In 1754 a Wesleyan chapel was built in the village and this has been in continuous use as a place of worship to this day.

Like many great men Wesley was somewhat small of statue, and to give him height as he preached he stood on a stool. The wooden stool originally used by Wesley in Osmotherley, a rough but strong block about six inches high, is kept as a prize possession by the Osmotherley Civic Society.

The Cross and Stone Table, C 1900

OTLEY

Otley has been described as "a quaint and old-fashioned town" doubtless with some justification, but perhaps the most important contributions it has made to the world is in the work and skill of its master craftsman and cabinet-maker Thomas Chippendale. Nobody was certain that Chippendale was born here until records were discovered of his birth and baptism in 1718. His father was a humble joiner and Thomas might also have remained undiscovered and obscure if he had not attracted the notice of the Earl of Harewood who became his patron and sent him up to London to be apprenticed as a cabinet-maker. Thomas rose steadily in skill and fame. In 1749 he set up his own workshops in Long Acre. His catalogue entitled "The Gentleman and Cabinet-maker's Directory" spread his name all over England and Europe. He worked mainly in mahogany and, though he employed a number of apparently disparate stylistic elements, those of the Classical style, the Rococo and "Chinoiserie", his work always remained quite distinctively Chippendale, among the finest and most beautiful craftsmanship in wood that the world has to show.

River Wharfe

PICKERING CASTLE

Standing on a limestone bluff in a commanding position on the edge of the North Yorkshire Moors are the ruins of the once vitally important Pickering Castle.

Almost all the kings of the Middle Ages visited Pickering at one time or another, many of them in far from happy mood. Bolingbroke spent several days here before going on to depose the ill-fated Richard II; and Richard himself is said to have been held prisoner briefly in the Castle on his miserable journey to a mysterious end at Pontefract Castle. When Robert the Bruce invaded Northern England, Pickering Castle avoided destruction by the offering of hostages and by the payment of levies, though the lesson of weakness was learned, and from 1324 until 1326 Pickering was extensively rebuilt and strengthened, with stone walls instead of mere wooden defences.

Pickering Church also has something of interest for the visitor in the form of a number of frescoed panels painted in the fifteenth century. One of the most striking of these depicts the martyrdom of King Edmund, the ninth-century martyr. The King is seen in the process of being peppered by arrows at remarkably close range. This panel bears a close resemblance, in composition if not in style, to the painting "The Martyrdom of Sebastian" executed by Antonie Pallaiuolo, the fifteenth-century Florentine artist.

POCKLINGTON

Kexby Bridge, spanning the Derwent at Pocklington may now seem to be unassuming enough though the discerning eye will notice that it is one of the most attractive bridges in East Yorkshire with its three semi-circular arches, each of which incorporates successively projecting rings to give it strength. The bridge was built in about 1760 when Pocklington stood on the main road between Hull and York. Indeed, this road was a vital artery before the opening of the Canal in 1818. Kexby Bridge was a vital connecting link for, so important was the road that the section between Beverley and Kexby Bridge had been turnpiked in 1784, while the section between Kexby Bridge and Beverley was turnpiked in the following year. Turnpike trusts were formed by local bigwigs who had a vested interest in preserving and improving the roads. They recouped their outlay, and no doubt gained a handsome profit by charging tolls to travellers using the roads. There is an attractive toll house standing quite close to the bridge at Barmby Moor.

After the opening of the Canal the roads were for a time of less importance. With the canals came increasing trade and greater prosperity. Better drainage led to improved crops. As crops were exported coal began to be brought in. The traffic flows abundantly down the A1079 today, but Kexby Bridge continues to pay its tribute to the old days of the turnpike roads.

PONTEFRACT CASTLE

It is believed that Pontefract Castle was built by a certain Ilbert de Lacy during the late eleventh century. It has seen much action since the tragic murder of Richard II in the year 1400, after he had been deposed by the ruthless Bolingbroke.

The Castle was much involved in the fighting during the Wars of the Roses, and, during the Civil War, the wheel of fortune turned several times. At the beginning the Castle was firmly in the hands of the Royalists, and, in 1644 General Fairfax laid an unsuccessful siege, the Castle being relieved by a Royalist force from Oxford. However, the Parliamentarians soon returned in greater force and this time the Castle fell after three months. In 1648 the Royalists returned and retook the Castle. There was another siege, this time lasting for six months, before the Parliamentary forces finally gained the Castle for good.

Pontefract is, of course, the home of that well known disc of liquorice, the Pontefract cake. Pontefract cakes have been produced in the town since the seventeenth century, and, during the late nineteenth century — a piece of information that might cause Ilbert de Lacy to turn in his Norman grave — there was actually a liquorice factory within the Castle walls!

From an old print

QUEENSBURY

If you enjoy a good prospect you might visit the village of Queensbury which stands 1,130 feet above sea level. It has been claimed that on a fine day one can see the spire of York Minister to the North East, Ingleborough in the Dales National Park to the North, while, if one gazes West from Queensbury, one can even distinguish Blackpool's famous tower!

The historical fortunes of Queensbury have been closely linked with the firm of John Foster and Son and with its remarkable protege, The Black Dyke Mills Band. There was a small reed and brass band in Queensbury as early as 1816, a year after the Battle of Waterloo, the chief horn player being a certain John Foster, later to become known as "Old Foster, the money man". As the fortunes of the band waned, so the star of John Foster and his brother William ascended. Fosters were to become the largest worsted manufacturers in the world, and, in the Great Exhibition of 1851, they took first prize for fabrics in alpaca and mohair and received a gold medal for yarns.

The band was taken over officially by the firm and became the great Black Dyke Mills Band, famous among musicians and laymen throughout the world. In 1860 the Band won for the first time the National Open Championships but this was merely the first of a score of such wins.

May the band, like real Yorkshire Pudding and Cricket, continue to flourish!

RICHMOND

One of the oldest theatres in England is Richmond's Georgian playhouse, built in 1788. In 1962, though the theatre had been closed for over a century, it was restored and reopened to the considerable joy of all theatre historians and other Thespians.

Richmond, made famous by the eighteenth century song "The Lass of Richmond Hill" is, indeed, a most attractive town, situated on the banks of the Swale. Its castle, built in the eleventh century, stands on a precipitous slope with a magnificent view across dales into the Vale of York.

This market town, for many centuries the largest corn market in the whole of England, was raised to the status of royal Borough by Edward III In 1329. An obelisk 65 feet high, first established in Henry VI's reign and rebuilt in 1771, proclaims itself the focal point of the rounded market place. On Saturday, market day, two fifteenth century halberds are placed outside the residence of the Clerk of the Market, The Mayor.

Each night from the medieval church of Holy Trinity by tradition the curfew is sounded.

RIEVAULX ABBEY

Three and a half miles north west of Helmsley, in a beautifully secluded
and well-wooded locality, stand the noble ruins of the Cistercian
monastery of Rievaulx Abbey, or "Rye Vallis" after the valley of the
River Rye. It was established in 1131 by Walter Espee, under the
directions of Saint Bernard of Clairvaux.

Because of the difficulties presented by the terrain, the Abbey was built
in a somewhat unorthodox manner for, instead of lying from east to west,
its central aisle was laid in a north to south position.

The chief glory of Rievaulx architecturally is its magnificent choir of
stone-ribbed vaults, built in 1225.

The monks of Rievaulx were most industrious in coaxing the
surrounding countryside to yield to their efforts and bear fruit. They
introduced arable farming into the valleys, whilst, on the limestone hills,
vast sheep walks were brought into being.

Best known among the abbots of Rievaulx is the saintly third abbot,
Aelred, who was canonized in 1191. It was Aelred who chronicled the
"Battle of the Standards" in which the Scots were defeated near
Northallerton in 1138. Aelred also carried out missions to the Galloway
Picts and even persuaded one of their chiefs to become a monk.

RIPLEY

In the middle of this village whose houses are mainly of French design stands a cobbled square with an old market cross and a stocks placed so that the malefactor might languish on the lowest step of the plinth and receive such punishment in kind as the villagers thought fit to mete out in the form of rotten vegetables and bad eggs. Other more sinister punishments are remembered in Ripley for it was against the walls of the Church of all Saints, after the battle of Marston Moor, that Cromwell had a number of Royalists executed.

The churchyard contains some items of historical interest, including the remains of a Weeping or Kneeling Cross.

Not far away stands Ripley Castle, the fine old ancestral home of the Ingilby family where they have lived since 1350. Here at Ripley Castle such distinguished figures as Oliver Cromwell and James I have stayed as guests. The Castle contains many treasures, including a collection of fine old furniture, some excellent paintings, and an assortment of weaponry from the Civil War.

It is a grim thought that while his Royalist opponents were suffering their grim fate outside All Saint's Church, Cromwell may have been putting his feet up at the Castle!

Stocks and Market Cross

RIPON CATHEDRAL

The main feature of Ripon architecturally speaking is its Cathedral, and the oddest feature of Ripon Cathedral is that it stopped being a cathedral for one thousand, one hundred and fifty years and then, in 1836, resumed its function.

The Norman Cathedral building was begun in the twelfth century but even this was built on the site of an earlier Anglo-Saxon church dedicated to Saint Wilfrid in 661 A.D., the crypt of which still survives beneath the central tower of today's Cathedral. This Anglo-Saxon crypt is of special interest since it is the last surviving remnant of a church that was only the eighth stone building produced by the Anglo-Saxon world.

Although Ripon was raised to a Bishopric in 681 A.D. this privilege was peremptorily withdrawn after only five years, and was not renewed until 1836 when Sir Gilbert Scott was commissioned to carry out the necessary renovations.

Another interesting aspect of Ripon's somewhat chequered ecclesiastical career is that the Norman structure was pulled down at the turn of the thirteenth century by order of Roger, the current Archbishop of York.

Perhaps the most interesting and impressive feature of this large, spacious and mercifully uncluttered Cathedral is the fifteenth century choir screen wonderfully proportioned and of symmetrical design.

RIPON

"Except Ye Lord Keep Ye Cittie, Ye Wakeman Waketh (or Watcheth) in vain." This has been Ripon's commendable town motto since time immemorial. In the Middle Ages the Mayor was also designated Wakeman or "he who watches". Even in the twentieth century the Mayor's horn-blower "sets the watch" every night at 9.0pm. by blowing the ornamental buffalo horn. Today this is simply a matter of tradition yet one is reminded of the Middle Ages when it was quite a different story. The Wakeman was, in these days, actually responsible for law and order in the city. Should a house be broken into during the hours of darkness, he had the responsibility of making good the loss, an honourable yet somewhat awesome task!

In the Middle Ages Ripon was a clothing centre of the first importance. It was also unique in the area as a centre of lace-making, a craft reputedly established by refugee nuns. Lace-making unfortunately died out about one hundred years ago with the death of the last surviving craftsman.

One should visit the Wakeman's House, an impressive fourteenth century residence, now serving as a museum. Also note the ninety foot obelisk which stands in the centre of the Market Square as a memorial to one William Aislabie who served the constituency as its member of parliament for sixty years, a truly prodigious feat!

The Forest Horn

ROBIN HOOD'S BAY

Nobody who was touring the coastal areas of Yorkshire could possibly
wish to drive in land without first visiting Robin Hood's Bay where streets
are scarcely more than footpaths giving enough room for fishermen to pass
with baskets on their backs, and where pantiled dwellings crowd, taking
advantage of every piece of level land on the steep chalk cliffs. The village
lies in a deep cleft where every available space must be utilized, and, in the
past, it has been the practice to build in the backgardens of houses to
accommodate the next generation.

Fishing has not been the only occupation of the inhabitants of Robin
Hood's Bay, as one might guess. For many years the village was a thriving
centre of smuggling, an enterprise that was carried on with little attempt at
concealment. During the days of the salt tax even that commodity was
smuggled into Yorkshire through Robin Hood's Bay.

A difficult question to answer is the question as to how the village got
its name. Who Robin Hood, that highly mobile character of legend and
myth, really was nobody can say. It is claimed, however, that he had a bolt-
hole in the Bay, and this might be considered as tactically wise, since,
when he was hard-pressed by his pursuers, though presumably not the
Sheriff of Nottingham on these occasions, he and his men might easily put
to sea with less chance of capture.

ROSEDALE

The village of Rosedale Abbey, now something of a tourist centre, enjoyed its one industrial boom when the ironstone mines flourished during the nineteenth century. During that time there were something like two thousand miners in the village. However, the mines fell into decline and were gradually closed down between the First and Second World Wars. For a hundred years Rosedale Chimney had provided a well-known landmark, but now even that has gone, leaving only a few derelict remains in the form of eight arches, viewed to best advantage from across the valley. Winter in Rosedale tends to be hard, the bitter North-West wind sweeping straight down the Seven valley and filling it with snow. With the collapse of the mining industry, the cottages of the miners gradually disappeared and it was not until after the Second World War that people with a few pounds to spare began to see the value of a country cottage, after which many of the half-derelict cottages received a new lease of life. Rosedale Abbey is beautifully misnamed. There has never been an abbey on the site of the village that was built in the reign of Henry II. However, it was named in good faith for there was a nunnery no longer now extant, though much of its old stone work remains as part of the village church of Saint Lawrence.

Church of Saint Lawrence

RUDSTON HOUSE

Whatever else the village of Rudston may have to commend it, it can boast that it is the birthplace of a distinguished writer, for it was here, at the end of the last century that Winifred Holtby, that most Yorkshire of writers was born.

Even as a girl Winifred Holtby began to show her literary gift and her mother, ever watchful for her talent, collected her small poems without her knowledge and had them printed under the title of "My Garden" by a firm of Hull printers in 1911.

After leaving school in 1916 Winifred spent a year nursing in the South of England before going up to Somerville College, Oxford in 1917. Her studies at Oxford were interrupted by a year's service with the W.A.A.Cs in France, but, after this, she returned to her degree in modern history.

Winifred Holtby's first novel "Anderby Wold" published in 1922 naturally showed much of the immaturity of youth, though the discerning eye could already distinguish an unusual talent. Already Winifred had started on a career of brilliant journalism, and Lady Rhondda invited her to join the staff of "Time and Tide", of which she was very quickly to become a director.

Her two novels, "Mandoa, Mandoa" and "South Riding" were written in the face of increasing pain and in defiance of the illness that was to bring about her death. Like many writers who have endured much suffering, she seemed to derive spiritual strength from her pain. "Mandoa, Mandoa" established her as a novelist both here and in America, while "South Riding", her major achievement, proved the culmination of her work.

RUDSTON STONE

In the middle of the village churchyard of Rudston, rising with a kind of fearful potency among the miniaturized gravestones, is the tallest standing stone in Britain. Rudston Stone projects some twenty-five and a half feet high. It is six feet wide and two and a quarter feet thick. Its weight has been estimated at approximately forty tons. Speculation suggests that there is as much of it below ground as there is above.

Nobody can now be certain how the Rudston Stone came to be erected in Rudston Churchyard. It is certainly much older than the Norman church beside which it stands. Its probable date is from 1600 to 1000 B.C. Legend attributes its placing to the Devil just as legend names the monoliths at Boroughbridge "The Devil's Arrows".

Can it be that the site of Rudston Church has been a sacred site for thousands of years? Is it possible that the early Christians came to Rudston with the deliberate intention of stamping out the old religion, and that they chose the sacred site of the older religion to challenge it and to defeat it there? Could it be that they intended originally to move the giant phallic symbol from its resting place in the churchyard but that ironically they found the task too difficult?

We know that the older pagan religion of the Druids survived, and still survives to this day, but the older faith became discredited and was looked down upon as the worship of the Devil. Little wonder, then, that the placing or Rudston Stone is attributed to the Devil!

SEATON ROSS

Few men can have had stranger obsessions than William Watson who lived
at Seaton Ross near the village of Market Weighton in the nineteenth
century. When he died aged 73 in 1857, the epitaph was cut onto his
headstone according to his own instructions:—

"At this church I so often with pleasure did call

That I made a sundial upon the church wall."

William Watson constructed three giant sundials in his lifetime, one for the
church, mentioned in his epitaph, one for his farm, and the one that is still
attached to the front of the cottage at Seaton Ross, its diameter being
twelve feet.

In the churchyard is another interesting grave, that of Margaret Harper,
who, during her lifetime, was accused of being a witch. She also wrote her
own epitaph, calculated to make her accusers aware of the planks in their
own eyes:

"The faults you've seen in me, strive to avoid;

Search your own hearts, and you'll be well employed."

Sundial

SCARBOROUGH

Scarborough is now a first class holiday resort, one of the largest between Aberdeen and Southend, offering every reasonable facility and enjoying a well-earned reputation. Yet, if one stands on the Marine Drive near the East Pier during a stormy winter's day, looking towards the sea through half-closed eyes, one can, perhaps, imagine that a thousand years have been rolled back for an instant and that the square sailed longships of Kormak and Thorgils are riding through the billows towards the shore. It was in 966 A.D. that the sleek ships of the Norsemen came with their formidable pagan warriors looking for a place to build a stronghold. According to the "Kormakssaga", an old Icelandic tale of the tenth century, the stronghold later set up was called Skarthiburg or "the place of Skarthi, the hare-lipped one", Skarthi being the nickname of Thorgil, the leader of the band.

This was only one of many incursions into the North-east by the Horsemen and Vikings, who came as pirates and raiders, but who, liking the country so much, settled and made it their home.

SCARBOROUGH CASTLE

After defeating the Scots at the Battle of the Standards near Northallerton in 1138 A.D., William le Gros, Earl of Albemarle, who had led the Yorkshire barons in the fight, decided to build a castle on the commanding height overlooking Scarborough. The site he chose had been well-used, the first recorded settlement having been in the Iron Age. The Romans had built a signal station there during the latter part of the occupation in 370 A.D. when their empire was being assailed by the Barbarians from the North and East. Like the nine lookouts of the Count of the Saxon Shores in Sussex it was primarily to give warning to garrisons further inland of the approach of Saxon raiders. The Roman lookout consisted of a square tower within a bastianed curtain wall.

Part of the square keep of the Norman castle still stands, rising to eighty feet and giving an impression of the castle's formidable presence in earlier times. The Castle, which figured prominently in the reign of King John and was also visited by Edward I and Richard III, has withstood five seiges. Indeed, in the Civil War, despite being heavily bombarded, it held out as the only Royalist port on the East coast until 1645.

During the reign of Charles II, the Quaker, George Fox, endured considerable hardship in the Castle as a prisoner before being released thanks to the merciful intervention of the King.

SELBY ABBEY

Most visitors to Yorkshire in search of sites of historical interest may well be drawn to the romantic ruins with which the county abounds. However, it should not be forgotten that many of the oldest and most impressive sites are still in use. Selby Abbey, for example, has an almost unbroken history of Christian worship, going back to the eleventh century and dating from approximately 1100 A.D. when William I was encouraging monastic life under Norman abbots in order to control the religious life of the North.

The rule of Benedict, indeed the very foundation of monasticism, had been introduced into Britain by the establishment of the Benedictine Abbey of Glastonbury in 940 A.D.

Although Selby Abbey somehow managed to survive the Dissolution intact, its history has not been altogether without misfortune. In 1690 the central tower collapsed and had to be rebuilt. In 1906 a terrible fire raged within the nave, destroying practically all the old work. The building was, nevertheless, restored in tasteful accordance with the concepts that inspired its Norman originators.

The Abbey, which dominates the main street of Selby, has some excellent features, including some very fine fourteenth centry stained-glass windows, but perhaps most interesting of all is the famous West Doorway, a richly ornamented example of the late Norman style.

SEMERWATER

Semerwater was made famous to the children of an earlier generation by the "Ballad of Semerwater" in which the poet William Watson retold the legend of a beautiful city that disappeared beneath the flood because it had failed to give succour to a beggar. Perhaps, as one looks out across those still, gleaming waters on a quiet and calm day one can almost give credence to the story. However, Semerwater has given up some of its treasures for, in 1937, when the water level fell by two feet because of dredging in the Bain, some interesting archaeological remains were revealed: wooden piles from ancient lake dwellings, pieces of bone, flint implements, and bronze spearheads of a particular quality, apparently abandoned in an emergency, probably during a sudden flood after heavy rains on the fells. Floods have been known in more recent times. In 1908, for example, cottages in Bainbridge were awash. On the other hand, in 1929 the whole of the Lake was completely frozen over so that moter vehicles could be driven upon it.

Beside Semerwater stands the Carlow Stone, an ice-borne boulder that attracts local couples who are about to marry. According to superstition to touch the Carlow Stone is lucky, bringing both prosperity and many children. Whether you desire both or neither it is as well, perhaps to identify the Stone before going too close to the Lake. Also keep your secrets to yourself since voices have an extraordinary ability to travel on Semerwater.

SETTLE

Closer inspection of the sign which has puzzled visitors to Settle for many years reveals that the man depicted is not in fact naked at all. Holding a heavy medieval plane before him, he appears to be ensconced in a coffin, at the base of which is an "X" frame chair. The initials "I.C." beneath the date 1663 give rise to the speculation that this may originally have been the sign of a local chair and coffin maker.

Settle has long been regarded as the capital of North Ribblesdale and is the focal point of one of the most beautiful and spectacular areas of the country, including rock features that are probably without parallel in Britain. The miniature peak of Castleberg towering over the houses has once or twice given rise to anxiety among the local inhabitants. In 1883, for example, two boulders came crashing down from the heights, one landing in the school yard and the other coming to rest behind the Congregational Chapel.

The word Settle comes from the Saxon "setl" or "a seat", and, during its heyday in the seventeenth century Settle was in fact a seat of greater importance than either Bradford of Sheffield. Its staple industries included hand-loom weaving, stocking knitting, tanning, hat-making and the manufacture of base coins. However, when the poet Thomas Gray visited it in the eighteenth century its prosperity had declined. Nowadays, it is a very pleasant market town.

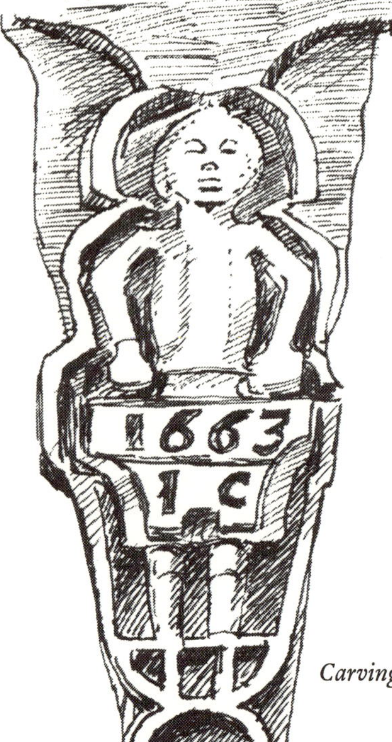

Carving above "Ye Olde Naked Man Cafe"

SHEFFIELD

Few but the most fanatical defenders of twentieth century utilitarianism
would dare to claim that Sheffield, the fifth city in England, has any
pretensions to beauty. However, the seeker after historical evidence would
be unwise to despise it as a possible source. It was here in the late
eighteenth century that a certain enterprising man, one Benjamin Hunts-
man, invented the crucible steel-making process, a method which was to
prove the foundation of Sheffield's dominance as a city of steel. Hunts-
man's process was used effectively up to the outbreak of the Second World
War.

One can still see the Cutlers' Hall in Church Street with its imposing
Grecian facade, and at Endcliffe Park, two and a half miles West of
Sheffield there is a cutler's grinding wheel dating from the late eighteenth
century. Most interesting of all, historically speaking, is the Abbeydale
industrial Hamlet Museum three and half miles south-west of the City.
Here one can see a number of interesting relics, including an old steel
furnace and some water-powered tilt hammers and grindstones.

If one wishes to move further back in time one can visit The Bishops'
House in Meersbrook Park. The Bishops' House, now a museum, reputedly
the home first of John Blythe, Bishop of Salisbury (1494-1499) and later
of Geoffrey Blythe, Bishop of Lichfield and Coventry (1503-1533), is
claimed to be the most complete example of a timber-framed house in
Sheffield.

The Cathedral

SKIPTON

Skipton Castle was the family seat of that famous Yorkshire family the Cliffords, which included the "Shepherd" Lord of Barden Tower and Lady Anne Clifford, well-known for her acts of benevolence and charity as well as for her lavish style of living. To George de Clifford, the Third Earl of Cumberland, is credited the Shell Room in the Gatehouse. George, a much travelled man, brought back quantities of shells and corals with which the room was decorated. His travels, no doubt the source of much of his wealth, involved a good deal of piracy, and, during one of his "campaigns" he captured Puerto Rico, but had to withdraw again when five hundred of his men died of sickness.

Skipton itself, as the parish registers testify, has known much sickness, particularly in the years between 1600 and 1700 when there were many ravaging epidemics of plague, typhus, and smallpox, When the castle was besieged from 1642 onwards the number of deaths in the town rose by over two-hundred and fifty per cent primarily because of disease introduced by the armies.

It is recorded in the register that, on July 22nd, 1665 William Wade, riding up from London to visit his father at Kilnsey, died on Rombalds Moor and, since his death was presumed to be of the plague he was buried there instead of being taken to his father's village.

    The Castle

SLEDMERE

The Georgian Age was the age that saw the beginnings of modern
agriculture, in which the old medieval system of dispersed holdings on
common fields and grazing rights on marginal land disappeared from most
places for ever. Thus many acts of enclosure were passed, particularly
affecting Yorkshire which was one of the most progressive areas in the
Country. Some landowners seized the opportunity to enrich themselves at
the expense of the poor but among the wisest and most forward looking
was Sir Christopher Sykes of Sledmere who transformed the Wolds from a
relatively unproductive sheep-grazing area into a land of milk and honey
lush with golden grain. The monument to Sir Christopher raised in West
Heslerton church in 1801 puts it thus:
"Every plan of improving the general state and surface of the country,
either by Enclosure, Drainge, Building, or Navigation, found in him an
active friend and supporter; in fact in every sense of the word he proved
himself an enlightened country gentleman. Whoever now traverses the
Wolds of Yorkshire, and contrasts their present appearance with what they
were, cannot but extol the name of Sykes".

Sledmere House, built in 1751, is still in the hands of the Sykes family.
It contains some fine examples of English and French furnishings, and is
set in gardens designed by that most famous of all improvers, Capability
Brown.

SNAPE CASTLE

The presence of even a substantial manor house on this site is surprising
for the word "Snape" means "mire" or "bog" and Ralph FitzRanulph, who
built the castle in 1250 must have been regarded as either extremely bold
or as a mild eccentric. However, whichever it was, it paid off for Snape
Castle still stands and most of its dilapidation is the result of human
neglect. Sir Ralph had twelve huge oaken piles sunk into the ground before
work commenced and this proved so effective that they remained
preserved in the peat until seven centuries later when a modern sewage
system was installed.

Snape Castle had provided a home for both the Nevilles and the Cecils.
Perhaps the best known resident was Katherine Parr, King Henry VIII's
last wife, the only one to survive him. Before being the wife of Henry,
Katherine had been married twice, the second time to Lord Latimer, and
she spent eleven years as his wife at Snape Castle. Little now remains as
evidence of her presence in the Castle though there is a small rubble-filled
room that is reputed to be her sewing-room. Also, as one might expect, her
ghost is said to haunt the castle. The five years she spent with Henry after
Latimer's death in 1542 can scarcely have been ecstatic. She died in
childbirth after being married to Thomas Seymour, her fourth husband,
for only a year. He survived her by one year, having his head cut off
for treason.

SOWERBY HALL

Sowerby Hall, a large Georgian mansion built by John Greane between 1714 and 1720, with later additions in 1808, stands in fifty acres of grounds and attractive old English walled gardens. The building is now utilized as a museum and chief among its exhibits are trophies, awards and mementoes of that distinguished woman aeronaut Amy Johnson, all presented to the museum by her father.

It was while she was in London that Amy was invited to the house of a friend close by Hendon Aerodrome. This was what inspired her to join the London Aeroplane Club and led subsequently to her gaining, not only her "A" pilot's licence but also her "C" licence in aeronautical engineering.

One can imagine the surprise and horror of her parents when she announced that she intended to become the first woman to fly solo to Australia, but on May 5th, 1930 she took off from Croydon in her 100 horse-power De Havilland Moth, painted green with the name "Jason" on the engine cowling.

What a flight that must have been! Finally landing to a tumultuous welcome Amy discovered that she had achieved world fame! The "Daily Mail" presented her with a cheque for £10,000 and she received the C.B.E. at the hands of King George V.

At the outbreak of the Second World War Amy, who would probably have preferred to fly combat aircraft, was employed ferrying fighter planes from factory to airfield. On the 5th January, 1941 she came down in the Thames Estuary. The body of this bravest of British women aviators was never recovered.

STAITHES

The fishing village of Staithes nestling down by the sea between towering cliffs was once a flourishing port as the name Staithe or Quay implies. The more important part of the village, known as Seaton, stood on the cliffs above, but, at the end of the Middle Ages, the fishermen began to move closer to the sea to avoid the daily climb up narrow cobbled streets.

Many of the local people can trace their ancestry back to the Vikings as the name Hansen, common locally, testifies.

Of particular historical interest is the traditional bonnet worn by the womenfolk as far back as anyone in the village can remember. Attractive they undoubtedly are, these bonnets were never intended primarily as adornment. When every man in the village was a fisherman, every woman served as a baiter, carrying her basket full of bait down to the harbour on her head and sometimes returning with her "skeel" or water-tub full of water from the beck. The bonnet was designed to protect the head and to facilitate the carrying her basket full of bait down to the harbour on rolled into a ring and worn above the cap to support the basket or "skeel". The flap at the back of the bonnet prevented water from dripping down the lady's neck. It is said that one could tell whether a lady was married, widowed, or single from the colour of her bonnet, an indication, perhaps, that limpets and mussels occasionally concealed a sweeter and more seductive bait!

Traditional Bonnets

STAMFORD BRIDGE

The village of Stamford Bridge on the River Derwent once played a significant role in History for it was here on Sunday 24th September, 1066 after a march that has been described as "one of the greatest feats of military manoevre in medieval history" that ill-fated King Harold, the last of the Saxon kings, took his brother Tostig and the giant Hardraada of Norway by surprise and totally defeated their army.

Hardraada, no doubt seeking a meeting with representatives from the Wolds, the Vale of Pickering and the Vale of York, went to the strategically placed Stamford Bridge. It was a hot day, and not expecting trouble, many of Hardraada's followers had discarded their protective jerkins, or burnies. Harold, having received news of Hardraada's invasion, hurried north. Learning of the meeting at Stamford Bridge, he pushed on. The first Hardraada knew of this was when Harold's forces appeared over the gentle rise between Stamford Bridge and Great Hemsley. Hardraada's forces, disposed on both sides of the river, were ill prepared for battle.

There was a short parley, during which Harold generously offered Tostig back his earldom if he withdrew. When Tostig asked Harold what he would do for Hardraada, Harold made his famous reply: "seven feet of English earth, or perhaps a little more as he is something tall". Harold kept his word for Hardraada was killed in the first phase of the battle.

STOODLEY PIKE

If you want an excellent view over the Calder Valley visit Stoodley Pike which stands on the edge of the tableland one thousand, three hundred feet above sea-level. "Pike" of course simply means summit and the monument gracing this particular pike was erected in 1814 to mark the Peace of Ghent after the fall of Napoleon at the Battle of Waterloo. However, this was by no means the first edifice on the site and there were certainly the ruins of an earlier structure standing where Stoodley Pike was erected. Indeed, legend claims the hill as a burial place of chieftains and human bones are said to have been unearthed when the excavations were carried out before the raising of the new monument. The obelisk raised in 1814 did not last long for within forty years it had collapsed. At the end of the Crimean War another obelisk was raised on its foundations. Further repairs were carried out in 1889 when a lightning conductor was installed.

Though scarcely inspiring as a feat either of architecture or engineering, Stoodley Pike does provide an excellent focus and destination for many an interesting walk.

The Monument

SWALEDALE

There is evidence that lead mining has occurred in the Dales from the Bronze Age until comparatively recent times. The Romans used lead for their plumbing work, for pipes, for cisterns, etc, and, after the Brigantes had been defeated at Stanwick Fort, many of the prisoners whre taken to the lead mines as slaves. The Saxons also used lead to cover the roofs of churches, for coffins, and also for plumbing. It is recorded that between 1179-1183 approximately 50 tons of lead were transported from Swaledale for the roofing of Waltham Abbeyy, and also for Clairvaux Abbey in France, from whence it was shipped via Boroughbridge and York, and thence by water to Rotterdam.

Mining was mostly on an inefficiently organized scale, the mines being scarcely big enough to admit more than one man at a time. Improvements in the mines occurred slowly as men were employed to sink new shafts or to drive levels. The tools of the miners remained very simple: a pick, wedges, hammers, etc, with leather sacks to contain the bouse and sledges that were wound to the surface by jack rollers. Wages were usually extremely poor and miners averaged little more than 12 shillings per week even as late as 1870.

Lead mining reached its peak with the boom period from 1840 to 1850, but by the end of the nineteenth century there were very few mines still operating and most of these had ceased work altogether by 1914.

SWINSTY HALL

There are still people who give credence to the power of the witches in
Washburn Valley. Many of the old stories of witchcraft centre round
Swinsty Hall and the rather eerie Timble Gill where the witches of the
seventeenth century had their rendezvous. Swinsty Hall was owned by a
man named Henry Robinson who was reputed to have killed a former wife
with witchcraft. Robinson, it seems, was closely involved with the Timble
Gill coven, the moving spirit of which was a certain Jenny Dibb whom he
employed as a housekeeper. Dibb had a familiar spirit in the form of a cat
called Gibbs. Robinson's near neighbour, Edward Fairfax, a relative of
General Fairfax who played such a significant role in the Civil War,
accused Robinson of witchcraft because of some difference of opinion
that had led to a law suit. Using a man from outside the parish as a hirer,
Robinson employed the witches to bewitch Fairfax's daughters, Helen and
Elizabeth. On Thursday 30th May, 1621 Helen Fairfax was abducted by
the witches and borne away to a great gathering of some forty witches at
Bank Slack. What they intended to do is not clear for, hearing that she had
been taken, Fairfax set off in reckless pursuit. Helen was rescued and, after
the rescue, Fairfax swore that she must have been carried off by some
magical power since she had travelled such a prodigious distance in such a
short time. Six of the witches came eventually to trial in York, but such
was Jenny Dibb's skill that they were soon released.

The Robinson family continued to occupy Swinsty Hall until 1722, and
there is still a rowan tree close to the house that is said to have the power
to cure warts.

Washburn Valley

114

THIRSK

Thirsk can boast several interesting historical buildings. For example, Thirsk Hall in Kirkgate, an eighteenth century house with a number of ornamental fireplaces and fine plasterwork is well worth a visit. Also the parish church of St Mary, begun in 1430 and sometimes referred to as "The Cathedral of North Riding" is of interest. Its tower has eight bells, the oldest dated from 1410.

Among the well-known figures connected with Thirsk is John Gilbert Baker, the Victorian botanist. The town has also made a valuable contribution to the national game, cricket, for George Macaulsey, the famous Yorkshire and England cricketer was born here, as was Thomas Lord, the founder of Lord's cricket ground.

One of the most interesting historical relics, however, is found at Ingramgate on the road to Easingwold. This is an old triangular milestone depicting a weary traveller resting upon his staff and motioning to his dog. It would be pleasing to be able to identify the dog as an Airedale terrier, a breed developed in Bingley for hunting along the River Aire. Alas, however, the dog on the milestone resembles more closely a somewhat sheepish Irish wolfhound.

THIRSK

When people think about cricket they usually also think about Yorkshire. They also, of course, think about the M.C.C. and Lord's Cricket Ground, and many people, doubtless, associate the name Lords with the aristocratic gentlemen who indulged in the game during the eighteenth and nineteenth centuries. In fact, Lord's Cricket Ground owes its existence to the business acumen of the Yorkshireman Thomas Lord who was born, as far as it can be established, at 14, Kirkgate, Thirsk on 23rd November, 1755. Lord was no aristocrat. His father had, in fact, been reduced to poverty by an injudicious political alignment during the Jacobite Rebellion.

When Thomas was young the family moved to Norfolk, and it was there that Thomas began to evince a special interest in cricket. There are conflicting tales of his prowess, some suggesting that he specialized in slow underarm bowling and others ascribing to him a fierce and devastating overarm action. Arriving in Islington, London, in 1780 he quickly became associated with the White Conduit Club. The Club was badly in need of a permanent ground, and Lord, backed by the Earl of Winchester and the Duke of Richmond, applied himself to the task of finding one. Several sites were employed temporarily before Lord managed to fix upon the present Lord's Cricket Ground on 22nd June, 1814. By this time the White Conduit Club had changed its name to the more felicitous Marylebone Cricket Club or M.C.C.

The Birthplace of Thomas Lord

THORNE LOCK

Water has played a vital part in the development of South Yorkshire and its rise to prosperity ever since the men of the Middle Ages strove to navigate the Don. By the end of the seventeenth century Rotherham and Sheffield had already become thriving centres of industry, but, as the pressures of expansion were felt at the beginning of the eighteenth century, it became a matter of some urgency that the river be rendered navigable throughout the year. By act of parliament work commenced from the year 1726 onwards. There followed the period now known as "canal mania" which lasted until the 1840s and which produced approximately sixty miles of canals connecting the Sheffield and Rotherham areas to the Humber, thereby opening up the South Yorkshire coalfield and ensuring its success throughout the period known as the Industrial Revolution.

Although the development of the railways effectively put an end to canal building, the canals continued to be used, and, indeed, continue to be used to this day. One can still see trains of "Tom Pudding" barges moving slowly up the canal and passing through Doncaster Lock on their way to the power station beyond.

Up at Thorne the canal has been employed in other ways: the building of light pleasure craft and even of larger sea-going vessels. The affluence of the twentieth century is reflected in the marina, where the young disport themselves in nimble plastic craft and rubber dinghies.

TICKHILL

The small town of Tickhill near Doncaster has quite a lot of historical interest to recommend it to the visitor. First there is the eighteenth century Market Cross, known as "The Buttercross", a domed structure supported by eight Tuscan columns. Nearby stands the medieval hospital of St Leonards, one of South Yorkshire's very few remaining timber framed houses, built in the fifteenth century. There are also other buildings of note within the town, including a fine church and a friary founded in 1260.

In the town centre stands Tickhill Castle, built in the twelfth century from stone on the site of a castle originally built of earth and timber. It is recorded that Richard the Lionheart gave lordship of the castle to his brother John, one of the least popular of the kings of England. The Castle has seen a good deal of action. As well as being besieged twice during Richard's reign, it also held out for three weeks against the rebellious Thomas Earl of Lancaster in 1322. During the Civil War it was held alternately by each side and the keep was probably destroyed at the end of hostilities to neutralize the castle. Though the gatehouse, still a splendid ruin, is visible from the road, the Castle is now in private hands and is not normally open to the public.

The Buttercross

118

TOPCLIFFE

The village of Topcliffe, once a centre of considerable importance, situated on the River Swale, approximately four miles South West of Thirsk has a rich and varied history. For example, on April 15th, 1603 the Scot who was about to become King James I, "The wisest feel in Christendom", rested for a night on his journey south for his coronation, at the home of Mr Wm Inglebye — a happy occasion. Less fortunately, his son Charles I was later handed over by the Scots to a committee of Parliament for a ransom of £100,000 in the Old Tollbooth, before being conveyed south to his trial and execution.

In the church is an excellent example of Flemish craftsmanship in the form of a brass memorial portraying Thomas de Topclyft and his wife.

It was in Topcliffe that the infamous Yorkshire witch, Mary Bateman was born in 1768. After a diabolic career of swindling, extortion, and poisoning, she was hanged in 1809. Even while awaiting execution in York, she told a fellow prisoner who had been deserted by her lover that she would melt down a guinea piece and form it into a charm, which, sewn into her stays, would infallibly lure him back. So great was Mary's power over the gullible that many maintained after her death: "She mun come again", a prophecy which has fortunately not been realized!

WAKEFIELD

It may seem, when one first considers the matter, strange that anyone should wish to build a church on a bridge, but that is exactly what Edmund of Langley did at Wakefield in 1350 A.D. or thereabouts. It is, in fact not quite as unusual as it may sound for there are four surviving bridge chapels throughout the country. Nor is the position so surprising when one considers that the number of wayfarers who must pass across a bridge during the course of a year must guarantee the incumbent a substantial congregation, at least in principle.

The Chantry is, indeed, a beautiful example in the Decorated Style at its most ornate and profuse. Above the three narrow pointed doorways are five bays, each containing a work in relief within a rectangular panel. From left to right, the subjects of the reliefs are The Annunciation, The Nativity, The Coronation of the Virgin, The Resurrection, and the Ascension.

This splendid reminder of the Middle Ages has not always been respected as a church. Before it was restored about one hundred years ago, it had done service as an old-clothes shop, as a library, as a corn-factor's office, and as a cheese-cake shop. When it was restored, the original facade was transferred to Kettlethorpe Hall. What one sees today is an exact and well-executed copy. However, the Chantry is now what it was intended to be, a fully operational church, for which we have to thank Edmund of Langley.

The Chantry on the Bridge

WENTWORTH WOODHOUSE

The vast eighteenth century mansion built for Thomas Wentworth, first Marquess of Rockingham has an immense frontage of six hundred feet, the longest, it is claimed in the whole of England. Wentworth Woodhouse is really two great houses joined together.

The West House, completed in 1734 and designed by a disciple of Vanbrugh is in the extravagant rocco style that one would expect. The larger and more ambitious Eastern House was designed by Henry Flitcroft, the master of the Palladian style. Though begun in 1730, work was still in progress on the interior of the building as late as the 70s. With all its variety and controlled splendour, this represents the apex of Flitcroft's work. It includes a curving stairway by Adam that rises from the pillared hall to a forty foot high Marble Saloon.

The park, within which the mansion stands, is itself full of a variety of attractions, including a bear-pit and a number of follies.

The Eastern House is currently occupied by the Lady Mabel College of Physical Education.

WHEELDALE MOOR ROMAN ROAD

Just south of Goathland one can still see the remains of a Roman road that runs over Wheeldale Moor and on for three miles to Stape. This is only the small surviving section of a Roman road known as Wade's Causeway that began at Malton and crossed the Vale of Pickering and the North Yorkshire Moors to end at the coast somewhere near Whitby. At Cawthorn, just north of Pickering it passes four Roman army practice camps, the remains of which can still be seen along the edge of the tabular hills. These practice camps are thought to have been built by the Ninth Hispana Legion which was stationed permanently at York 9or Eboracum) after the defeat of the Brigantes during the reign of Trajan (98-117 A.D.).

It is well-known that the Romans always built their roads as straight as possible, through cuttings and along the sides of hills. They used whatever local materials were available: stone, pebbles, flint, even clay. The road on Wheeldale was surfaced with rammed gravel, but this has long since disappeared, leaving only the large rough stones on which it was laid and the drainage culverts beside it.

WHITBY

Facing the sea but with an eye on the ruins of Whitby Abbey stands the statue of one of Yorkshire's greatest sons, Captain James Cook, Under his left arm he holds appropriately a rolled up map, while, in his right hand, he grasps his nautical compasses.

Cook was one of the best possible kinds of explorer, a man of insatiable curiosity and great courage, armed with the weapons of peace. When young he lived further up the coast in a pink cottage by Staithe Harbour, working as a draper's apprentice in the town. Later he moved to Whitby which is justifiably proud of him, for it was out of one of Whitby's yards that "The Endeavour" came, and it was from Whitby that Cook sailed on the first expedition to the South Seas in 1768.

Every schoolboy knows how Cook shielded his sailors from the ravages of scurvy by keeping a supply of fresh fruit and vegetables aboard ship. Fewer, perhaps, have appreciated the remarkable degree of accuracy which he attained in his maps.

His house in Grape Lane is marked with a plaque.

WHITBY ABBEY

Approached by a stairway of one hundred and ninety-nine stone steps, the most famous monastery of the early church, the Abbey of St. Hilda, founded in A.D. 657, stands above the town of Whitby on a headland of the Esk, an impressive ruin built in sandstone of contrasting hues.

The Abbey was first built by St. Hilda as a Benedictine foundation for both monks and nuns, on land donated by Oswry of Northumbria to celebrate his victory over the pagan King Penda of Mercia.

It was here that the famous Synod of Whitby healed the division between the two rival factions within the English Church in 663 A.D., a decision being reached to accept the usages of Rome and to devise an acceptable method of fixing the date of Easter. It was here also that Caedmon received the vision that caused him to turn from his humble employment as lay brother and cowherd to become the first English religious poet, and "Father of English Sacred Song", finding inspiration in the dramatic stories of the Old Testament.

The Abbey built by St. Hilda has, of course, disappeared long ago, destroyed by the Danes in the ninth or tenth centuries. However, the Normans were not slow to rebuild. Essentially the ruin is a notable example of early English architecture built on earlier foundations. It contains some excellent detailed carving and a number of windows of the later Decorated Period.

WORSBROUGH

The village of Worsbrough near Barnsley, together with Worsbrough Bridge and Worsbrough Dale, contains many buildings of historic interest, including its ancient church, a fine old vicarage and Worsbrough Hall, an early seventeenth century building. At Worsbrough Dale stands the late Tudor building of Rockley Old Hall.

Most visitors to Worsbrough are drawn to the Old Corn Mill which has been renovated by the South Yorkshire County Council and is now preserved as a working mill museum. There was a mill recorded at Worsbrough in William the First's Domesday Book. The present building, however, dates back to the seventeenth century though it also has a number of early nineteenth century additions. It contains, among other features of interest, an enclosed wheel in perfect working order and also a very early internal combustion engine for "stand by" use. The Mill stands below the dam which, in earlier days, fed the Deane and Dove Canal via a feeder which was used to service the Worsbrough Colliery, thus connecting it with the South Yorkshire canal system. The dam still exists though the stream which used to connect Worsbrough to the Deane and Dove Canal is no longer navigable. Some slight compensation at least for the modern fisherman is that it is now well-stocked with fish.

YORK

York Minster, or, to give its full title, The Metropolitan Church of Saint Peter, is said to be the largest Gothic Church in England. The magnificent throne of the Archbishop of York, situated just inside the Choir near the entrance from the South Aisle, and possessing a vaulted roof with a central boss in the form of an archiepiscopal mitre, bestows upon the Minster the status of a Cathedral. As the mother church of the whole of the Northern Province of the Church of England, 'ministering' to the people, its title of "Minster" is most fitting.

There is evidence of a Christian church in York as far back as the Roman occupation but, when the Romans returned to Rome to defend their homeland from the attacks of the Barbarians in the fifth century, the Church of York became moribund. It was revived some two hundred years later when King Edwin of Northumbria became converted. Immediately Edwin had a wooden church erected on the site and this is now marked by the Font, whose wooden cover was designed by Sir Ninian Comper. Paulinus, to whom Edwin owed his baptism, was consecrated the First Bishop of York.

The first Norman Cathedral, traces of which are still to be seen in the crypt, was begun by Archbishop Thomas of Bayeux between 1070 and 1100 A.D., but the present gothic structure was not completed until the later end of the fifteenth century.

One of the features of York Minster is its giant bell which, it is claimed, has the deepest and richest tone of any bell in Europe.

The Minster

YORK 2

Approaching York from the South, the Kings of the Middle Ages would enter the City by the Micklegate Bar, and, raising their eyes above the fine Norman arch to the tops of the twin towers they might see the heads of traitors impaled on spikes. Just above the arch to the left and right one can see the entrances to the barbican which was, alas, removed in the nineteenth century.

Although there had been a settlement of the powerful British tribe, the Brigantes, for centuries at York, it was not until after Quintue Petillius Cerialis, the Roman Governor of Britain decided to push north in 71 A.D. and discovered the easily defended position at the confluence of the Ouse and the Foss, that the building of York or Eboracum began. The soldiers constructed an earth rampart round their fortress, and it was to the south-west of this that the city grew up, quickly becoming one of the most important in the Roman Empire. Many Emperors visited York, and it was here that Constantine the Great, the First Christian Emperor, was declared. Fragments of the Roman wall can still be seen in the section from St Leonard's Hospital to the Multangular Tower.

The city was, of course, enlarged during the Middle Ages, and much of the wall, dating from the thirteenth century, can still be walked upon today. A number of fine bars or gates remain in an excellent state of preservation, including Walmgate Bar which is the only one in England with its barbican intact.

Micklegate Bar

YORK 3

The Vikings have often been cast in the role of the villains of history and
have been associated with pillage and rape, perhaps somewhat unfairly as
the record of York suggests. It was in Northumbria that many of the
Vikings decided in 876 to settle and become farmers, and later traders,
making Jorvik (or York) their capital city. For nearly one hundred years
York was almost exclusively a Viking city, as recent excavations by the
York Archaeological Trust of the Coppergate site have shown. The very
name Coppergate (or Coopergate) "the streets of the wood turners"
betrays its Viking origins as do many of the other street names in the city.

The excavations have shown that York in the time of the Vikings
consisted mostly of wooden buildings with a few stone buildings going
back to Roman times. Many artefacts have been discovered, including
coins, iron utensils, bronze pins and brooches, and glass beads, as well as a
variety of leather goods, all suggesting a settled community with trading
links with Dublin, another important outpost of Viking culture, as well as
with Scandinavia and beyond. York was in fact one of the most important
Viking trading centres in Europe.

YORK 4

Considered by many to be one of the best preserved medieval streets in
Europe and described in the official guide as "York's most romantic
street", the famous Shambles attracts many visitors every year. In the
Middle Ages this street was known as "The Fleshammels", or "The Street
of Butchers", and today one can still see shelves in front of the shop
windows with hooks above for the butchers to display their meats. The
overhang of the buildings ensured that for the greater part of the day the
carcasses were shaded from the sun. Indeed, these timber-framed houses
lean so close that one can shake hands across the street from some of the
upper storeys. No. 40 is still preserved as "The Butchers' Hall" and No. 35
was the home of Margaret Clitherow, the butcher's wife who was later
canonized by the Roman Catholic Church as Saint Margaret of York. In
1586 she was pressed to death under a heavy door, on which were piled
stones, because she had hidden a Jesuit priest in her house. The house
stands now as a chapel to her memory.